LEARNING TO LOVE LITERATURE

LEARNING TO LOVE LITERATURE

PRESCHOOL THROUGH GRADE 3

LINDA LEONARD LAMME, EDITOR
University of Florida

National Council of Teachers of English
1111 Kenyon Road, Urbana, Illinois 61801

Grateful acknowledgment is made for permission to reprint the following material: "Let's Pretend" from *Listen and Help Tell the Story* by Bernice Wells Carlson. Copyright © 1965 by Abingdon Press. Used by permission. "Old Shoes" by Irma S. Black from *Read Me Another Story,* compiled by the Child Study Children's Book Committee at Bank Street College.

NCTE Editorial Board: Paul T. Bryant, Marilyn Hanf Buckley, Thomas J. Creswell, C. Kermeen Fristrom, Jane M. Hornburger

Book Design: Tom Kovacs, interior; Gail Glende Rost, cover

NCTE Stock Number 27878

Library of Congress Cataloging in Publication Data

National Council of Teachers of English. Committee on Literature in the Elementary Language Arts.
    Learning to love literature.

    Includes bibliographies.
    1. Childrens literature—Study and teaching (Primary) I. Lamme, Linda Leonard. II. Title.
LB1527.N37   1981   372.6'4   81-14076
ISBN 0-8141-2787-8   AACR2

CONTENTS

LIST OF FIGURES

INTRODUCTION

In the fall of 1977 the Committee on Literature in the Elementary Language Arts met to consider their charge from NCTE to develop materials to help early childhood teachers see literature as central to the curriculum. This book is a result of our deliberations over a three-year period. At first we considered compiling a booklist of children's books suitable for integrating into curricular areas. That approach would have helped teachers who wanted to supplement their instruction with literature. But our charge from NCTE went further than that. What about teachers who wanted to make literature central to their entire curriculum, not just a frill tacked on as an afterthought? More and more teachers of young children are seeing that isolated instruction in basic skills does not bring with it the interest, excitement, and learning that sharing literature in meaningful contexts generates. More teachers are seeking alternatives to rigid instruction from basals. This book provides an alternative. Teachers seeking to put more meaning into their curriculum can begin gradually by bringing more literature into their instruction. The ultimate goal, however, is a completely integrated curriculum with literature as its base.

As our committee planned this book, we rejected the "readings" approach where each author writes a chapter and there is little continuity from one topic to another. If we seek to help early childhood teachers integrate curriculum, our approach needs to be well organized, logical, and comprehensive, for although teachers are often encouraged to share literature with young children in the instructional setting, few guidelines are available for using literature as the core of the curriculum. This often results in a literature curriculum that is spotty, incidental, and ill defined. This text presents the point of view that literature can be the core of an early childhood curriculum, a place to start, not just a pleasant addition to a theme of study or a way to fill in slots of time.

We begin with theory. The first chapter presents our rationale for making literature an integral part of the early childhood curriculum. We present some goals for the appreciation, comprehension, and extension of literature in the curriculum.

The second chapter moves from theory to practice. The first thing a teacher must do to integrate literature into the curriculum is to create a literature-rich classroom environment. A reading corner can be far more than a collection of books. In addition, it is important to provide a broad collection of props to enhance the literature curriculum. Young children need multiple encounters with the same story (through puppets, flannelboards, dress-ups, and the like) in order to internalize the story structure, language, and content.

Once the teacher has created a stimulating environment, teaching strategies must be employed to expose children adequately to literature. Although there are books available on storytelling, few early childhood teachers actually tell stories to their classes on a regular basis. For that reason, concise directions are given in chapter three for storytelling and choral speaking. In many classrooms young children occasionally encounter literature, but typically the only routine with literature is the teacher reading aloud. The literature habit can be fostered by other classroom literature routines, such as SSR (Sustained Silent Reading). At the end of this chapter a "classroom literature routine inventory" allows the teacher to stand back and assess the degree to which literature is routinely encountered in his or her room.

The fourth chapter takes one literature routine, reading aloud, which has repeatedly been shown to have a substantial impact upon young children, and thoroughly explores this impact. Lap reading with one child is seen to be essential to a good early childhood classroom. Lap reading is such a critical technique for helping children learn what reading is all about that it behooves teachers of young children to recruit other adults or older children to sit down individually with prereaders and beginning readers to share literature together. The "reading aloud to children scale" at the end of the chapter provides a second self-assessment for teachers. They can check on their abilities to present literature orally in a manner in which children are not only entertained, but also informally taught.

Each curricular area is briefly explored for literature opportunities in chapter five. The bibliographies accompanying each section should be especially helpful to teachers. This chapter contains the central theme of the book—that literature can be an integral part of all curricular areas. Specific examples of how eight teachers have accomplished this are found in chapter six.

Chapters seven and eight suggest resources that can enhance the literature curriculum. First, human resources are discussed. To provide individual attention for each child plus a rich and rotating repertoire of encounters with literature, volunteers are needed in the classroom. Further, the classroom teacher can accomplish only a limited amount with each child. If parents work with teachers, however, learning is greatly enhanced. This is especially true in the area of literature, where lifelong literature habits are so greatly determined by the home environment.

As was mentioned previously, young children respond positively to multiple exposures to the same piece of literature. Chapter eight gives teachers numerous outlets for enhancing their literature curriculum through media.

The summary chapter restates the purpose of the book and presents an example of how many curricular areas can be "webbed" around one book. Whether teachers choose to integrate many books into a theme or let the themes evolve from a book, as is done here, literature achieves a status it is not currently being accorded in basic skills classrooms. Assessing a child's progress via a standardized test is a very narrow and limited practice. The book concludes by asserting the importance of documenting children's progress in a literature curriculum in far more meaningful ways than merely administering tests.

By the end of the book, teachers will have had the opportunity to establish goals, create a stimulating literature environment, perfect their teaching strategies, provide a variety of resources, and evaluate the results of their literature program. Teachers who have explored literature in such great depth will have a hard time limiting their instruction to basals. They will at the least supplement basal programs and at the most teach basic skills through a meaningful integration of those skills into the literature curriculum. It is the hope of the authors that our readers will become aware of the potential of literature as a natural integrator of content and process.

1 THE LITERATURE CURRICULUM

Vivian E. L. Cox
University of Arizona

Why a Literature Curriculum for Young Children?

Bringing books and children together is part of our cultural heritage. It is a tradition which begins in the cradle through the sharing of nursery rhymes, lullabies, bedtime stories, fingerplays, and poems. The story told, the verse recited, the book shared—all are part of the child's first literature curriculum. It is a curriculum rich with pleasant associations: a soft lap, a warm bath, a snuggly bed—delightful sounds, memorable language, melodious rhythms—intriguing characters, mysterious settings, magical happenings—familiar themes, varying moods, and differing styles. This initial literature curriculum makes possible the impossible, uses common words in uncommon ways, titillates the senses, nurtures curiosities, stretches the memory, and triggers the imagination. The seeds of literary appreciation sprout as young children and literature come together.

There are many children who come to school with the benefit of a rich literature background. However, other youngsters come to their first classroom lacking these warm, rich literature experiences. Some children have been deprived of books at home. Television, outdoor play, games, visiting, and accompanying a parent on errands may have usurped the place of books for these children. While these other experiences can be wholesome and necessary activities, they necessitate scheduling of reading times which many families don't provide. For children from these families in particular, the early childhood teacher must provide a planned literature curriculum, not just the occasional reading of a book.

Early literature experiences are as basic to children's development as any other type of nourishment. Through these experiences children's knowledge of the lore and language of literature begins to develop. Children's acquaintance with Mother Goose, "The Three Bears," and "Red Riding Hood" prepares them to meet Curious George, Winnie the Pooh, and many other literary characters. A sense of story begins to emerge. The ear is attuned to the rhymes and rhythms of literary language. Children become familiar with books—the way pages turn, how print moves from left to right and then skips back to left again, what a written word is, how to recognize key words in the story, and some basic sight words. Exposure to literature provides experiences that enhance reading readiness, (1) developing a knowledge of literature, (2) character development, (3) a sense of story, (4) language development, and (5) beginning reading skills that help children acquire a literary storehouse. Children will develop "metalinguistic awareness," or a sense of what printed language is all about. Without "metalinguistic awareness" or literary storehouse, all the basic skills instruction in the world will not make any sense. Reading and writing skills will be memorized, but they will not be understood and applied. Our central concern, then, is to help the teacher bring children's literature into the mainstream of the curriculum so that each student will acquire not only a love for literature, but also a storehouse of literature-related information that will provide a solid foundation for future learning.

Goals of a Literature Curriculum

A literature curriculum provides a base of affective as well as cognitive development. Children naturally learn many things while enjoying this multifaceted, multimedia resource. Books, films, recordings, as well as other persons, serve as avenues for literary sharing and exploration. If the literature curriculum is viewed as the totality of children's experiences with literature rather than a course of study, horizons are expanded that allow children to truly become "involved" with books.

General goals of an early childhood literature curriculum include the following: (1) provision of pleasure, (2) nourishment of the imagination, (3) promotion of creative expression, (4) development of imagery, (5) presentation and exploration of a variety of styles and forms for the communication of ideas, (6) awareness of the functions of language, and (7) acquisition of metalinguistic awareness. These goals permit children to sample, taste, devour, or reject literary offerings, while at the same time to learn an incredible amount about the world we live in.

Within the early childhood literature curriculum, these goals are integrated within three areas: (1) appreciation, (2) comprehension, and (3) extension. These goal areas are interdependent, requiring a balance of emphasis that is best achieved by "planned experiences" with literature. Planned experiences with literature for young children begin with an awareness of the potential of literature as a source for both affective and cognitive development. Literary resources become the instructional core, not a supplement to text materials. Ensuring opportunities for literary experiences requires systematic planning to make selections and develop activities that center upon content as well as process for the achievement of particular curricular goals. The end result of such planning is linguistic and literary richness—a marvelous legacy for children to bring to the writing and reading arts. "Ideally, children will have many experiences with stories and poems read or told to them during the time they are learning to be independent writers and readers. If the experiences are pleasurable and if literature is made an important and natural part of their environment, it is likely that children will establish positive attitudes towards reading and literature that will remain with them throughout their lives" (Sims, 1977).

Appreciation

Appreciation is the first and most important goal area of an early childhood literature curriculum. Appreciation, in this instance, means developing the sensitive awareness of children to those features of the literary experience that personally appeal to them. Appreciation is based upon enjoyment of the experience as children sharpen their discriminating perceptions in terms of content and literary artistry. Whether it be just the "fun" of the experience, the beauty of illustration or language, a fascination with the world of fantasy, the solving of a problem, or some other motive, children must desire to be part of the literary sharing. The seeds of literary appreciation germinate in the years before school for many children. The in-school literature curriculum should continue to nurture this appreciation and help those who have not yet acquired a love of literature develop it.

Children appreciate books for many reasons. Reading books for some children has always been a pleasurable experience. They will anticipate continuing literary experiences that are pleasant. Sharing books in a warm, supportive situation is crucial to helping children "feel good" about the material shared. Thus, the time and the setting as well as the literary choice all contribute to the value of the experience.

Humor as a Basis of Appreciation

Appreciation of many books begins with the fun of the tale. Humor is the hook that catches children, that makes them participate in the literary experience, and won't let them stop until the experience is complete.

Humor is readily found in collections of riddles, conundrums, and other brain teasers. Cynthia Basil's *Nailheads and Potato Eyes* presents elementary riddles that use parts of the body, with dual meaning, as the answers. The fun of this book is in the guessing—a self-initiated test in which children take great delight. Examples of other books involving humorous language manipulation for the young are *Ghastly Ghostly Riddles* by Gloria D. Miklowitz and Peter Desbery and *The Six-Million-Dollar Cucumber* by E. Richard Churchill.

Printed versions of folk songs and folktales are replete with humorous incidents. *I Know an Old Lady* by Rose Bonne is a print version of the folk song involving an old woman who swallowed an unusual collection of animals in her stomach in an effort to catch "the spider that wiggled and wriggled and jiggled inside her." Other books using folk songs as humorous bases are *Go Tell Aunt Rhody, Clementine,* and *She'll Be Comin' 'round the Mountain,* all by Robert Quackenbush. *Yankee Doodle* by Edward Bangs and illustrated by Steven Kellogg and *Old MacDonald* illustrated by Robert Quackenbush, also provide a humorous base for appreciation. These books and others are appreciated by children for one major reason. They're fun!

Imagery as a Basis of Appreciation

Language which conjures up mental images helps children to visualize both the known and the unknown. Such language paints pictures with words. There is an appeal to the auditory senses that develops listening skills ranging from the perception of sound to comprehension of imagery. Whether children have made underwater explorations or not, they are still able to understand and to visualize the sights of the ocean depths when the language of Swimmy is shared:

> . . . a lobster who walked about like a water-moving machine.
>
> . . . a forest of sea weeds growing from sugar candy rocks.
>
> . . . an eel whose tail was almost too far away to remember.
>
> by Leo Lionni
> from *Swimmy*

Consider the mental images that could emerge from the following description.

> The wind howled over Alfalfa Hill. It ripped crisp leaves from the whipping trees. And hurled them crazily, crazily. They cracked and scraped and nestled, covering the forest floor. Quiet, quiet it drifted down. Whisper. Hour after hour it fell.
>
> by Peter Parnall
> from *Alfalfa Hill*

Additional references utilizing provocative language that lends itself to the "creation of images in the mind" include *The Tomten and the Fox* by Astrid Lindgren, *The Moon Jumpers* by Janice May Udry, and *The Fire Bird* by Toma Bogdanovic.

Format as a Basis of Appreciation

Children often appreciate books that "work" in different ways. The format of the book itself often lends itself to pushing, pulling, turning, matching, or providing the missing piece. In *Zoo City* by Stephen Lewis, young children are asked to match machinery commonly found within the city with zoo animals. In this split book format, the top half has the machinery and the bottom half the animal. As children look through the book, they attempt to match the pairs, such as a steam shovel with a giraffe. In *Houses Keep the Weather Out* by Jennie Soble, children take a tour of houses around the world, visiting igloos, castles, tents, etc. Then they are invited to complete the book by either drawing or cutting and pasting a picture of the particular house mentioned. Other books that use intriguing formats are *A See Parade* by Robyn Supraner and *My Very First Book of Colors* by Eric Carle.

Illustrations as a Basis of Appreciation

Appreciation can stem from the beauty and uniqueness of illustrations. For young children, illustrations help develop visual literacy. Pictures are as essential to the development of the child's visual imagination as words are to the development of verbal imagination. Pictures can serve as a basis for pictorial storytelling. Quality illustrations possess a power of their own to transport children to places familiar and unfamiliar. In *The Circus* by Brian Wildsmith, colorful illustrations bring the spell of the sawdust ring to young readers or listeners as the succession of acts loved by children are presented. Page after page, children are invited to enlarge and expand their vision of the circus through the magic of the illustrator's brush.

Paul Goble uses brilliant paintings that sweep across the page to illustrate *The Girl Who Loved Wild Horses.* The bold stylized illustrations tell the story and the details invite children to again and again "journey with the girl and the wild horses."

In *Snow White* by the Brothers Grimm, illustrated by Trina Schart Hyman, the struggle between good and evil is vividly portrayed. The magnetism of the illustrations invites children to raise many questions: Why is she doing that? What is happening here? Is that the way dwarfs really look? Why does the frame of the mirror change? How did the queen disguise herself to fool Snow White? What is a bier? These and other questions evolve as children respond to the pictorial images created. The drama of this tale comes to life through illustrations that are as enchanting for children as the story itself.

Marilyn Schweitzer uses photographs to bring animal tracks in the desert to children in Byrd Baylor's *We Walk in Sandy Places.* These illustrations subtly reveal the evidence of life in the desert by telltale tracks. The photo-artistry of Schweitzer results in warm brown illustrations that invite children to "read the tracks" like one reads a story.

Other books in which illustrations present the same magnetic appeal include:

Anansi the Spider by Gerald McDermott

Why Mosquitoes Buzz in People's Ears by Verna Aardema, illus. by Leo and Diane Dillon

The Wave by Margaret Hodges

Wake Up, Jeremiah by Ronald Himler

I Stood upon a Mountain by Aileen Fisher, illus. by Blair Lent

Ox-Cart Man by Donald Hall, illus. by Barbara Cooney.

Imagination as a Basis of Appreciation

Another mode of appreciation that attracts children to literature is represented by those books in which the improbable is rendered probable. The setting of such books is a world where magic works, unicorns and other imagined creatures really exist, and around the next corner you actually meet a witch or a dragon. Children are caught by the adventure, the conquest, and the excitement that can be theirs in this fantasy world. The only key into this world is that which unlocks the child's imagination.

In literature even a house can challenge the imagination, especially one like Baba Yaga's. Baba Yaga, a traditional figure in Russian folktales, lives in a most unusual house that moves through the woods on chicken legs and responds to the commands of its mistress:

> . . . "Izbushka, Izbushka, lower your door to me." The chicken legs of the hut, called Izbushka, bent to the ground and Baba Yaga climbed inside.
>
> by Ernest Small and Blair Lent
> from *Baba Yaga*

In another situation, children are introduced to a peaceful town in the country named Calabria. There they are introduced to an old lady called "Strega Nona," which is fine until they are told this means "Grandma Witch." Then they further discover:

> Although all the people in town talked about her in whispers, they all went to see her if they had troubles. Even the priest and the sisters of the convent

went, because Strega Nona did have a magic touch.

> by Tomie de Paola
> from *Strega Nona*

In such an imaginative world a she-dragon may seek a blacksmith's help in devising a way to lure a young boy to shore to be snatched and carried off:

> The she-dragon saw that she could do nothing, so she went to the blacksmith. "Smith, Smith, forge me a voice as fine as the voice of Ivanko's mother." And the blacksmith forged one. The she-dragon went to the shore and began calling: . . . And Ivanko thought, "Now that's my dear mother bringing me food!" So he paddled to shore. The she-dragon quickly snatched him from the boat and off she carried him.
>
> by Marie Halun Bloch
> from *Ivanko and the Dragon*

The traditional fairy tales of magic and adventure such as *Cinderella, Sleeping Beauty, Hansel and Gretel,* and *Jack and the Beanstalk* are in this mode. These books offer expanding horizons and a chance to venture into places that do not exist. Children grow in their ability to understand, enjoy, and create such imaginings through the power of the mind. For them, involvement with such literature results in an educated imagination.

Other books to be considered in the development of imaginative powers are *Liza Lou and the Yeller Belly Swamp* by Mercer Mayer, *The Three Robbers* by Tomi Ungerer, and *Where the Wild Things Are* by Maurice Sendak.

Empathy as a Basis of Appreciation

Some books are appreciated because they deal with a problem—either one common to most of us or one particularly common in the lives of young children. Most young children make mistakes at one time or another. It's important for them to discover that other people do this too. The fact that sometimes even mothers make mistakes is conveyed well by Judith Viorst in the following passage:

> My mama says there isn't any mean-eyed monster with long slimy hair and pointy claws going scritchy-scratch, scritchy-scritchy-scratch outside my window.
>
> But yesterday my mama said I couldn't have some cream cheese on my sandwich, because, she said, there wasn't any more. And then I found the cream cheese under the lettuce in back of the Jello. So . . . sometimes even mamas make mistakes.
>
> by Judith Viorst
> from *My Mama Says . . .*

Or consider the children who are called so many "pet" names by different people. How comforting it is to discover through a book such as *My Little Cabbage—Mon Petit Chou* that children around the world are fellow sufferers of such figurative endearments:

> I live in the United States, but that is not all . . .
>   My grandma calls me 'My little monkey—'
>   My mother calls me 'My little devil—'
>   My father calls me 'My little lamb—'
>   But this is the real me.
>
> by Susan Purdy
> from *My Little Cabbage—Mon Petit Chou*

The children who discover *If It Weren't for You* by Charlotte Zolotow or *My Brother Fine with Me* by Lucille Clifton not only discover characters who engage in wish-fulfillment regarding another sibling but also extend that discovery in terms of awareness of the possible consequences if one's wish is granted.

William also had a wish in *William's Doll*—a wish not understood by his father, his brother, or the boy next door. William wanted a doll. Wish-fulfillment in this instance was made possible by William's grandmother with the gift of a doll and her very wise words:

> He needs it to hug and to cradle and to take to the park so that when he's a father like you, he'll know how to take care of his baby and feed him and love him and bring him the things he wants like a doll, so that he can practice being a father.
>
> by Charlotte Zolotow
> from *William's Doll*

Oftentimes the child needs clarification of personal feelings. Just as frequently, help is needed to understand other people's feelings. A deeper understanding of human motives is an outgrowth of books such as *Amigo* by Byrd Baylor Schweitzer, and *Much Bigger Than Martin* and *Can I Keep Him?* by Steven Kellogg.

Other Sources of Appreciation

Still other sources of literary appreciation emerge from involvements with books that satisfy the curiosity of the child, tie in with the sense of adventure, provide information, challenge the mind, or present a unique literary style. The options for nurturance of literary appreciation are as varied as the children themselves. As teachers share a wide variety of good books with children, experiences with literature will develop children's tastes.

Comprehension

A second goal of a literature curriculum for young children is comprehension. Comprehension involves the capacity to understand what is heard and what is read. Comprehension grows into different levels. Youngsters enjoy listening to stories and developing a host of comprehension skills (sequencing, cause and effect, main idea, etc.) that they will later apply when reading on their own.

Too often young children think of reading as uttering the sounds of words. They get absorbed in word calling and forget there is content to a story. Steinbeck (1951) wrote: "The design of a book is the pattern of a reality controlled and shaped by the mind of the writer." We all have our own worlds of reality. So do young children. They can only approximate the author's constructed world to the degree that their own world of experience and that of the author overlap. Their ability to become involved in a story influences the degree of their understanding of this literary world and thus their degree of comprehension. Children are meaning-seekers. According to Applebee (1979) they use a range of social structures including stories as a way of structuring the everyday world. Through continuing and varied experiences with literature, children arrive at understandings concerning rules of language, thought, and behavior as their "sense of story" develops. Children also discover the basic elements of plot, characterization, setting, and style through their literary experiences. They develop an awareness of various literary forms and structures. Their knowledge of how a story works, along with ideas for authorship, evolve with each experience. Thus, comprehension as well as other basic skills are "caught," not "taught" through literary explorations. For young children, literature is not a course of study; it is a natural continuation of their own life experience—a means, not an end. Through personal involvement with literary materials children grow in these skills.

Literature leads the child beyond a single text or text series. Literary resources are numerous and rich in those elements that provide cues to help children comprehend. Textbooks, conversely, designed for instructional purposes tend to separate English out of the totality of language and divorce it from the realm of literature. Such materials can rob children of opportunities to develop and refine skills of comprehension.

Comprehension is much more than a matter of definitions. Comprehension is what children come to understand through their experiences with life and with books. Their conceptions and perceptions emerge, develop, and undergo refinements as they become sensitive to content and literary style. Facility with the sounds and rhythms of language, understanding of the ordering of language units, and the ability to reconstruct the author's meaning are key comprehension skills developed through a rich literature curriculum.

Comprehension of Literary Language

Comprehension skills grow in several areas as a result of literary involvements. One understanding that children develop quite early is that literary language, the language in books, differs from that used in spoken communication. As linguistic magicians, authors and poets play creatively with language when they use alliteration, onomatopoeia, metaphors, and other devices. As children are exposed to such magic, they respond to this creative playfulness and their own awareness and understanding of literary language grows and grows. Evidence shows that authors and children are quite alike in their use of language to express observations (Byers, 1977).

An adult poet has written:

The smell of this afternoon's rain
Is driving the flowers crazy—
They're screaming for me to kiss them!

> by Sam Hamod
> from *If Dragon Flies Made Honey: Poems*

A third grade poet wrote:

I like flowers.
   Blue flowers
   Yellow flowers
   Red flowers
I like flowers.
   Flowers in gardens
   Flowers in vases
   Flowers in trees
I like flowers.

> by Evelyn Wallace
> from *My Poem Book*

Both poets have expressed their feelings concerning flowers in distinctive literary styles. Each portrays mastery of the language in individual ways. Literary language is provocative, complex, and

highly structured. Comprehension as well as command of literary language requires many experiences with books such as the following: *Mud Pies and Other Recipes* by Majorie Winslow, *A Penny a Look* by Harve Zemach, and *Doctor Rabbit's Foundling* by Jan Wahl.

Comprehension of Other Language Skills

As children move into the world of print with increased independence, the benefits of a literature curriculum continue. Literature is the resource from which they receive "exposure to complex syntactic structures and diverse vocabulary not found in oral language, but which is found in most reading material" (McCormick, 1976). Reading or hearing literature promotes a feeling for beautiful imagery, rhythm, figurative speech, and cadence of our language. Literary experiences encourage children to go beyond basic language arts instruction. Following the models provided by literature, children become more verbal. They speak and write more maturely with expanded vocabulary and sentence patterns. As they grow in an awareness of themselves and the world, they also grow in their abilities to communicate with others.

Experiences with literature offer exposure to the rhythms of literary patterns. Children develop skills of aural literacy when a literature curriculum provides the opportunity to hear the language rhythms and patterns that authors create. They retrieve the language and patterns that are memorable for them. According to Whitehead (1968), "Children often recognize immediately a particularly melodious, rhythmic, or emotional word or phrase . . . and thousands of such language elements have been memorized instantly by children." Books such as *Alexander and the Terrible, Horrible, No Good, Very Bad Day* by Judith Viorst or *The Judge* by Harve Zemach contain patterns that young children may claim and use quite readily.

Aural literacy also helps the child to deal with the speech and vocabulary items that are rooted in our literary heritage. Our language is replete with words, phrases, and allusions thoroughly embedded in traditional literature. Think of the figures of speech that come from Aesop's fables: "sour grapes," "dog in the manger," and "the boy who cried wolf." Words and phrases from Aesop, La Fontaine, and others live forever in our language and are part of every child's literary heritage. The sharing of stories which contain figures of speech helps children develop an "educated ear." The total context of these stories allows children to figure out the meanings of such patterns. Oral experiences are an important part of the literature curriculum for children. When children have heard many stories and poems told or read, they acquire a framework for use of information. This word system is three-pronged: (1) Semantic—What makes sense?, (2) Syntactic—What would fit here?, and (3) Phonologic—What sounds belong here? This framework develops children's sensitivity to specific language and the ordering that propels the story onward, establishes tone, and provides sounds pleasant to the listener. Authors serve as models for children, who learn to paint literary pictures with words, first orally, then in writing.

Comprehension of Visual Symbols

Skills of visual literacy (or comprehending visual symbols that are not words) develop as children explore many books. Their comprehension of what a book is, how one works, and different ways to visually share their ideas is based upon many opportunities to explore books. Visual literacy skills include the ability to understand and comprehend a variety of symbols. As children explore the many resources of the world of literature, they discover a variety of visual symbols that help to tell the tale. They learn that pictures, numerals, abstract art, and alphabetic symbols are tools used by other authors and illustrators in their work. Experiences of personal authorship permit children to use these same tools to share their messages with others. Hence, children become not only consumers, but producers of literary works.

Literature serves as a base for both writing and reading. The works of Durkin (1972), Moss (1977), and Wilcox (1977) represent only a few of the studies that reveal the effects of literary experiences upon young children. Just as they draw upon other experiences to help them to communicate with others, so, too, do they draw upon literary experiences. They learn about writing by listening to the works of great writers. They grow in reading and listening abilities by developing strategies that help them understand the experiences, real or imagined, of others. They discover that written language in a literary form provides a structure upon which they can hang their own ideas and experiences.

Comprehension of Literary Elements and Structures

Literature, like oral language, uses both elements and structure to convey an idea. Comprehension of literature for children includes learning to deal effectively with these various elements and structures. Carefully planned experiences with literature can initiate a lifelong courtship that woos children with the language and the structure of the tale. In this courtship, children can discover the basic literary elements of plot, characterization, setting, and style while also increasing their awareness of differing literary structures. Thus, their "sense of literature" grows.

If one dragon story begins and ends:

> Everytime there was a full moon the dragon came out of his lair and ravaged the countryside. He frightened maidens and stopped up chimneys and broke store windows and set people's clocks back and made dogs bark until no one could hear himself think.

> When they reached the king's castle the people all leaped for joy to see that the dragon was dead, and the princess ran out and kissed the youngest brother on the forehead, for secretly she had hoped it would be him.

> by John Gardner
> from *Dragon, Dragon and Other Timeless Tales*

and another dragon story begins and ends:

> Once upon a time, in the ancient kingdom of Lyraland, there lived a good but lonely dragon named Harry.

> And that is the story of how Harry the dragon beat the knight, married Mabel Mae, got a good job in the post office, and lived happily ever after.

> by Walter Dean Myers
> from *The Dragon Takes a Wife*

then children learn literary and linguistic signals which tell them that even though both stories are about dragons, there will be important differences in their characters and thus in the nature of the tales. From their previous experiences with life and with literature, they have clues to understanding. Each dragon lives in a land of fantasy, but a dragon that ravages and frightens and winds up dead does not live in the same place as one who is "good but lonely" and winds up married and with "a good job in the post office." A child senses immediately that their stories (plots) will not be the same. Literary experiences develop comprehension of the characters and the settings of the story, but life experiences provide the personal perceptions and interpretations in all literary explorations.

Literature is an excellent resource for the development of comprehension skills. Your guidance and structuring of experience are valuable towards this end. But comprehension skills may also develop as the book itself becomes a teacher. The power and magnetism of the tale activate the child's need to know and to understand. A well-rounded literature curriculum assures children's involvement with books in a manner that aids in comprehension and development of language and literary skills.

Extension

The third goal area of an early childhood literature curriculum is extension. By extension we mean going beyond the story, a "stretching" of the book in ways that intensify children's understanding and enjoyment of the story and spark their desire to listen to stories and to learn to read. For young children, books are more than just stories. Characters become friends. Stories, rhymes, and parts of stories become part of children's knowledge storehouse to be used and reused in various ways.

There are many ways to extend literature—through direct experience, media, music and drama, art, and language. These types of extension experiences help children learn, get to know themselves, become more sensitive to language, expand their vocabularies, develop a sense, and develop oral fluency and visual literacy.

Limiting literary experiences in the classroom to reading aloud and silent reading deprives young children of many opportunities to dig deeper and grow more from books. To read a story once is a pleasant experience, but to read it many times, memorize parts, chant refrains, and "live it" in some way is to make that book, story, or rhyme an integral part of children's experiences.

Chapter nine outlines some specific ways teachers have helped children extend literature "beyond a book." Here we offer some general guidelines for and examples of story extension.

Direct Experience

We all know that direct experience is vital for young children. Children learn through their active participation in the experience. To always just read a book but do nothing before or after reading is to deprive youngsters of direct experiences that could enhance their literary experiences. There are times when just reading aloud to children is enough, but extending the book in some way will really make it come alive. We often neglect direct experience as an extension activity.

It's hard to read *Blueberries for Sal* by McCloskey and not desire to go berry picking. Fortunately, blueberries may be found in places other than Maine, so lucky children in many areas might have an experience with blueberries, too.

Pancakes for Breakfast, a wordless book by Tomie de Paola, is a story of how one little old woman managed to get pancakes for breakfast. This wordless picture story helps young children "learn" the ingredients necessary for a pancake recipe. A natural follow-up of this book is to make and eat some pancakes.

Everybody Needs a Rock by Byrd Baylor can lead to many experiences with rocks. You may decide to have a rock-hunting expedition with your students that will serve as an introduction to this book. The class might then compare their rock selection criteria with those of the author.

As you get tuned in to the idea of integrating literature and direct experiences, you'll find that the opportunities are endless. For each activity of your school day and for each subject in your curriculum, there are stories, rhymes, fingerplays, or songs that could accompany the activity. And for each book you share with young children, there are probably many direct experiences that could accompany it.

Media

A list of available media resources has been included in Chapter eight. Media provide an excellent way to extend literature. Not only can children enjoy a record, a cassette, or a film or filmstrip, they can also try producing their own songs and stories.

For example, to develop activities to accompany the book *Yankee Doodle* by Edward Bangs (illus. by Steven Kellogg), you might play the cassette (Weston Woods) as the children enter the room one morning. The next step might be to show the pictures in the book to a small group while the song is playing. Be sure to put the book and cassette in a listening center for individuals to hear and sing and read. Later in the day the children might enjoy marching around to the song (rhythm aids auditory discrimination, a readiness skill). For children who are beginning to read, the song could be written on chart paper. Since there are several versions of this story, exposing the children to another version (such as the one by Richard Shackburg) will give them an opportunity to compare books in terms of content. One version gives a recipe for hasty pudding that could be used in a cooking activity.

After visiting a farmyard, show the film or filmstrip of *Rosie's Walk* by Pat Hutchins. The children will enjoy seeing the fox get "outfoxed." Then leave the book in the book area for children to enjoy on their own. They'll know which way to turn the pages without a doubt!

Music and Drama

Books such as *London Bridge Is Falling Down* by Peter Spier, *Oh, A-Hunting We Will Go* by John Langstaff and Nancy Winslow Parker, and *Six Little Ducks* by Chris Conover provide many opportunities for extension. Not only may children "sing these stories," but each also lends itself to dramatization. Children may retrieve the rhythmic chant of London Bridge while "playing" this beloved game. Acting the role of hunters catching the fox to put in a box is a delightful experience for young children. You may wish to discover how your children will role play the six little ducks.

Try using background music to enhance the reading of many stories. Or invite children to "act out" a character or a scene from one of their favorite stories. The strong rhythmic language patterns of some books can inspire students to experiment by writing musical versions. Still other books may inspire dramatizations. "Stretch" some books by combining these two activities; music and drama are excellent ways to allow children to claim stories as their own.

Art

Art experiences provide another avenue for book extension. The variety of art materials available for use will inspire many book-stretching activities.

Georgie by Robert Bright may inspire ghostly pictures. Paints or transluscent crayons may be used for their creation. Tissue paper or kleenex ghosts have their own eerie quality; some children may prefer to create ghosts of this type. Whatever their choice of art material, your children's ghosts will help them remember Georgie, the friendly ghost.

Constructing houses of sticks, straw, and bricks helps to bring *Three Little Pigs* by William Pène du Bois to life. Paper bag or stick puppets might also be made for use in retelling this story. Let several children create dioramas or rolled murals that tell the story in sequence. So that children don't grow to think of wolves as evil, you might discuss the role of the wolf and rewrite the story with mythical creatures like a dragon in the wolf's role.

It Looked Like Spilt Milk by Charles Shaw or *Little Blue and Little Yellow* by Leo Lionni might inspire a "torn" paper activity. Let children tear white paper and create their own silhouette versions of this book. Or let them make tempera blottos and follow this by deciding what their blottos look like.

Everyone Knows What a Dragon Looks Like by Jay Williams could easily inspire dragon-making. Play dough, clay, or salt clay should produce some intriguing dragons as children pinch, twist, and shape their personal versions.

Just as there are numerous illustrative styles in literature for young children, there are complementary activities that might relate to each one. Crayon (Feodor Rojankovsky in *Frog Went A-Courtin'*), colored pencil (many of Taro Yashima's books), and collage (Lionni, Keats, and Carle) are especially good media for young children to use. Woodcut effects (Marie Hall Ets, Don Freeman in *Beady Bear*) can be achieved with sponges and styrofoam. You might investigate the kinds of media used to illustrate picture books (Cianciolo, 1976) and then develop your own activities to let your students experience similar media firsthand.

The art activities that may be designed as book-stretching experiences are as varied as the books available. Each experience helps children internalize the tale.

Language

Literature serves as a basis for the development of both oral and written language skills. Many different language experiences can be designed to encourage children to retrieve, explore, and extend the language of the book.

Many stories contain a repetition of words and phrases that children can chant as the story is read. Chanting is a means by which children become comfortable with the language of a story. This activity also provides a vehicle for the unlocking of print as children try to find the familiar refrain. Try sharing books such as *The Old Woman and Her Pig* by Paul Galdone, *The Judge: An Untrue Tale* by Harve Zemach, or *Alexander and The Terrible, Horrible, No Good, Very Bad Day* by Judith Viorst. Invite children to "chime in" when they "know" what the story will say. Show how some of these language patterns look when you write them on large chart paper. Children will be delighted to discover that they can "read" these parts.

Books without a printed story line (some may have one or two words) may inspire either oral or written language activities. Initially, children may only be able to provide a sentence or two for each page of the story. This is an important step, however, since it establishes the foundation for future elaborated storytelling experiences. Mercer Mayer's *One Frog Too Many*, Yutaka Sugita's *My Friend Little John and Me*, or John Goodall's *Paddy Pork's Holiday* are books without words that can be used to help children in their development of story lines. For vocabulary development try *Circus* by Brian Wildsmith or *Circles, Triangles, and Squares* by Tana Hoban.

Discussions of favorite characters will also sharpen young children's language skills. Whether it is Amelia Bedelia, Pippi Longstocking, or other characters, discussions encourage children to pose questions, reveal their insights, or invent other situations for characters. Can children tell about Amelia Bedelia's encounter with a motorcycle? Small groups or individuals could portray many humorous events that might give students insight into characterization.

The use of story starters, experiences in parallel plot construction, and the creation of story variations are types of activities that help students develop skills of personal authorship. For example, "Once upon a time there was a peddler who sold shoes . . ." might challenge the children to create a story comparable to *Caps for Sale* by Esphyr Slobodkina.

Summary

Extension of literary experiences creates the opportunity for children to grow in personal power and understanding. Children quite naturally engage in this goal of a literature curriculum. They bring all the experiences of their young lives to the literary setting. Such experience is the tool used to help children better understand themselves, and to understand those elements and structures that comprise the literary work. By listening to, reacting to, writing about, dramatizing, and responding to literature in various ways, children grow in their appreciation and comprehension of this resource. Each involvement activity facilitates their linguistic and literary development, expands their knowledge about the world, brings them closer to independent reading ability, and contributes to their lifelong involvement with books.

The remaining chapters contain many suggestions for continuing and expanding children's involvement with literature. They will give you ideas, provide resources, and suggest ways for you to strengthen your teaching skills in using literature.

Children's Book References

Aardema, Verna. *Why Mosquitoes Buzz in People's Ears.* Illus. Leo Dillon and Diane Dillon. New York: Dial Press, 1975.

Bangs, Edward. *Yankee Doodle.* Illus. Steven Kellogg. New York: Parents Magazine Press, 1976.

Basil, Cynthia. *Nailheads and Potato Eyes.* Illus. Janet McCaffery. New York: William Morrow & Co., Inc., 1976.

Baylor, Byrd. *Everybody Needs a Rock.* Illus. Peter Parnall. New York: Charles Scribner's Sons, 1974.

Baylor, Byrd. *We Walk in Sandy Places.* Photographs by Marilyn Schweitzer. New York: Charles Scribner's Sons, 1976.

Bloch, Marie Halun. *Ivanko and the Dragon.* Illus. Yaroslava. New York: Atheneum Publishers, 1969.

Bogdanovic, Toma. *The Fire Bird.* New York: Scroll Press, 1973.

Bright, Robert. *Georgie.* New York: Doubleday & Co., 1959.

Carle, Eric. *My Very First Book of Colors.* New York: Thomas Y. Crowell Co., 1974.

Churchill, E. Richard. *The Six-Million-Dollar Cucumber.* Illus. Carol Nicklaus. New York: Franklin Watts, Inc., 1976.

Clifton, Lucille. *My Brother Fine with Me.* Illus. Moneta Barnett. New York: Holt, Rinehart and Winston, Inc., 1975.

Conover, Chris. *Six Little Ducks.* New York: Thomas Y. Crowell Co., 1976.

de Paola, Tomie. *Pancakes for Breakfast.* New York: Harcourt Brace Jovanovich, Inc., 1978.

de Paola, Tomie. *Strega Nona.* Englewood Cliffs, N.J.: Prentice-Hall, Inc., 1975.

du Bois, William Pène. *Three Little Pigs.* New York: Penguin Books, Inc., 1970.

Fisher, Aileen. *I Stood upon a Mountain*. Illus. Blair Lent. New York: Thomas Y. Crowell Co., 1979.

Fisher, Aileen. *Once We Went on a Picnic*. Illus. Tony Chen. New York: Thomas Y. Crowell Co., 1975.

Freeman, Don. *Beady Bear*. New York: Viking Press, 1954.

Galdone, Paul. *The Old Woman and Her Pig*. New York: McGraw-Hill Book Co., 1961.

Gardner, John. "Dragon, Dragon" from *Dragon, Dragon and Other Timeless Tales*. Illus. Charles Shields. New York: Knopf Books, 1975.

Goble, Paul. *The Girl Who Loved Wild Horses*. Scarsdale, N.Y.: Bradbury Press, Inc., 1978.

Goodall, John S. *Paddy Pork's Holiday*. New York: Atheneum Publishers, 1976.

Grimm Brothers. *Snow White*. Trans. Paul Heins. Illus. Trina Schart Hyman. Boston: Little, Brown & Co., 1974.

Hall, Donald. *Ox-Cart Man*. Illus. Barbara Cooney. New York: Viking Press, 1979.

Hamod, Sam. "The Jealousy" from *If Dragon Flies Made Honey: Poems*. Collected by David Kherdian. Illus. Jose Aruego and Ariane Dewey. New York: Greenwillow Books, 1977.

Himler, Ronald. *Wake Up, Jeremiah*. New York: Harper & Row, Publishers, Inc., 1979.

Hoban, Tana. *Circles, Triangles, and Squares*. New York: Macmillan Publishing Co., Inc., 1974.

Hodges, Margaret. *The Wave*. Illus. Blair Lent. Boston: Houghton Mifflin Co., 1964.

Hutchins, Pat. *Rosie's Walk*. New York: Macmillan Publishing Co., 1968.

Kellogg, Steven. *Can I Keep Him?* New York: Dial Press, 1971.

Kellogg, Steven. *Much Bigger Than Martin*. New York: Dial Press, 1976.

Langstaff, John. *Oh, A-Hunting We Will Go*. Illus. Nancy Winslow Parker. New York: Atheneum Publishers, 1974.

Langstaff, John. *Frog Went A-Courtin'*. Illus. Feodor Rojankovsky. New York: Harcourt Brace Jovanovich, Inc., 1955.

Lewis, Stephen. *Zoo City*. New York: Greenwillow Books, 1976.

Lindgren, Astrid. *The Tomten and the Fox*. Illus. Harald Wiberg. New York: Coward, McCann & Geoghegan, Inc., 1965.

Lionni, Leo. *Swimmy*. New York: Random House, Inc., 1973.

Mayer, Mercer. *Liza Lou and the Yeller Belly Swamp*. New York: Parents Magazine Press, 1976.

Mayer, Mercer. *One Frog Too Many*. New York: Dial Press, 1975.

McCloskey, Robert. *Blueberries for Sal*. New York: Viking Press, 1948.

McDermott, Gerald. *Anansi the Spider—A Tale from the Ashanti*. New York: Holt, Rinehart and Winston, Inc., 1972.

Miklowitz, Gloria D., and Desbery, Peter. *Ghastly, Ghostly Riddles*. Illus. Dave Ross. New York: Scholastic Book Services, 1978.

Myers, Walter Dean. *The Dragon Takes a Wife*. Illus. Ann Grifalconi. Indianapolis: The Bobbs-Merrill Co., Inc., 1972.

Parnall, Peter. *Alfalfa Hill*. New York: Doubleday & Co., Inc., 1975.

Purdy, Susan. *My Little Cabbage—Mon Petit Chou*. Philadelphia: J. B. Lippincott Co., 1965.

Quackenbush, Robert. *Clementine*. Philadelphia: J. B. Lippincott Co., 1974.

Quackenbush, Robert. *Go Tell Aunt Rhody*. Philadelphia: J. B. Lippincott Co., 1973.

Quackenbush, Robert. *She'll Be Comin' 'round the Mountain*. Philadelphia: J. B. Lippincott Co., 1973.

Shackburg, Richard. *Yankee Doodle*. Illus. Ed Emberly. Englewood Cliffs, N.J.: Prentice-Hall, Inc., 1965.

Schweitzer, Byrd Baylor. *Amigo*. Illus. Garth Williams. New York: Collier Publishing Co., 1963.

Sendak, Maurice. *Where the Wild Things Are*. New York: Harper & Row, Publishers, Inc., 1963.

Shaw, Charles. *It Looked Like Spilt Milk*. New York: Harper & Row, Publishers, Inc., 1947.

Small, Ernest, and Lent, Blair. *Baba Yaga*. Illus. Blair Lent. Boston: Houghton Mifflin Co., 1966.

Soble, Jennie. *Houses Keep the Weather Out*. Lawrence, Mass.: Two Continents Publishing Group, Inc., 1975.

Spier, Peter. *London Bridge Is Falling Down*. New York: Doubleday & Co., Inc., 1967.

Sugita, Yutaka. *My Friend Little John and Me*. New York: McGraw-Hill Book Co., 1973.

Udry, Janice May. *The Moon Jumpers*. Illus. Maurice Sendak. New York: Harper & Row, Publishers, Inc., 1959.

Ungerer, Tomi. *The Three Robbers*. New York: Atheneum Publishers, 1962.

Viorst, Judith. *Alexander and the Terrible, Horrible, No Good, Very Bad Day*. Illus. Ray Cruz. New York: Atheneum Publishers, 1976.

Viorst, Judith. *My Mama Says There Aren't Any Zombies, Ghosts, Vampires, Creatures, Demons, Monsters, Fiends, Goblins, or Things*. Illus. Kay Chorao. New York: Atheneum Publishers, 1973.

Wahl, Jan. *Doctor Rabbit's Foundling*. Illus. Cyndy Szekeres. New York: Pantheon Books, 1977.

Wallace, Evelyn. "Flowers" from *My Poem Book*. Benson, Ariz.: Benson Primary School, 1976.

Wildsmith, Brian. *The Circus*. New York: Oxford University Press, Inc., 1979.

Williams, Jay. *Everyone Knows What a Dragon Looks Like*. Illus. Mercer Mayer. New York: Four Winds Press, 1976.

Winslow, Marjorie. *Mud Pies and Other Recipes*. Illus. Erik Blegvad. Macmillan Publishing Co., Inc., 1961.

Zemach, Harve. *The Judge*. Illus. Margot Zemach. New York: Farrar, Straus & Giroux, Inc., 1969.

Zemach, Harve. *A Penny a Look—An Old Story.* Illus. Margot Zemach. New York: Farrar, Straus & Giroux, Inc., 1971.

Zolotow, Charlotte. *If It Weren't for You.* Illus. Ben Shecter. New York: Harper & Row, Publishers, Inc., 1966.

Zolotow, Charlotte. *William's Doll.* Illus. William Pène du Bois. New York: Harper & Row, Publishers, Inc., 1972.

Professional References

Applebee, Arthur N. "Children and Stories: Learning the Rules of the Game." *Language Arts* 56 (September 1979): 641-646.

Byers, June. "Presenting Poetry." In *Literature and Young Children,* edited by Bernice E. Cullinan and Carolyn W. Carmichael. Urbana, Ill.: National Council of Teachers of English, 1977, pp. 78-84.

Cianciolo, Patricia J. *Illustrations in Children's Books.* Dubuque, Iowa: William C. Brown Co., Publishers, 1976.

Durkin, Delores. "Children Who Read before Grade One." *The Reading Teacher* 14 (January 1961): 163-166.

Lamme, Linda, and Kane, Frances. "Children, Books, and Collage." *Language Arts* 53 (Nov/Dec 1976): 902-905.

McCormick, Sandra. "Syntactical Complexity and Vocabulary Diversity in Two Groups of Children's Books." Report prepared at Ohio State University. ED 141 835. 1976.

Moss, Joy F. "Learning to Write by Listening to Literature." *Language Arts* 54 (May 1977): 537-542.

Sims, Rudine. "Reading Literature Aloud." In *Literature and Young Children,* edited by Bernice E. Cullinan and Carolyn W. Carmichael. Urbana, Ill.: National Council of Teachers of English, 1977, pp. 108-119.

Somers, Albert B., and Worthington, Janet Evans. *Response Guides for Teaching Children's Books.* Urbana, Ill.: National Council of Teachers of English, 1979.

Steinbeck, John. *The Log from the Sea of Cortez.* New York: Viking Press, 1951.

Stewig, John Warren, and Sebesta, Sam L. *Using Literature in the Elementary Classroom.* Urbana, Ill.: National Council of Teachers of English, 1978.

Whitehead, Robert. *Children's Literature: Strategies of Teaching.* Englewood Cliffs, N.J.: Prentice-Hall, Inc., 1968.

Wilcox, Leah M. "Literature: The Child's Guide to Creative Writing." *Language Arts* 54 (May 1977): 549-554.

2 SETTING THE STAGE

Marilou Sorenson
University of Utah

Early childhood teachers who want to make literature an integral part of their curriculum and not just an isolated experience of reading a book, need to examine their classroom environments carefully. The presence of certain props and materials will stimulate an interest in literature. The classroom atmosphere will have an impact. If children are expected to be quiet most of the time, working independently, with each child doing essentially the same task, literature is not likely to be shared and enjoyed. The opposite extreme, where children are aimlessly playing for most of the day won't stimulate high levels of thought and discussion about literature either. For literature to be the focus of an integrated curriculum, the teacher must plan systematically.

This chapter will give you ideas for creating a classroom environment in which the use of literature abounds. Chapter three will suggest specific techniques for using literature.

The Classroom Environment

Children learn through what they live and by what they do. To children the classroom can be a place to grow, expand, test out ideas and predict the outcomes of their questions. It is a place that Montessori called ". . . the liberty of pupils in their spontaneous manifestations." A prepared environment provides successful experiences for all children in a climate where ideas and creative learning can flourish.

A classroom that supports appreciation, comprehension, and extension of literature reflects a commitment to a goal of not only teaching children to read but helping them become readers. This commitment suggests time, space, and resources to explore books, extend ideas, and make responses. Daily experiences with literature are a starting point for developing a lifetime habit of reading.

A classroom that promotes the use of literature sustains individuality and independence of learning, interaction, and the integration of literature into an interdisciplinary approach to teaching.

Individuality and Independence of Learning

The teacher who realizes the worth of literature not only accommodates the differences that exist within the class but also helps the children make individual choices of time, materials, and actions. Each child's interests are considered, as well as the varied genres, in order to challenge multiple reading abilities in print and nonprint materials. The inherent possibilities that this diversity offers classroom instruction are limitless.

Interaction through Communication

In a stimulating classroom environment the process and interpretation of reading are as valued as the book that is read. As students read a story, they are encouraged to seek help when help is needed. Oral problem solving and dialogue are open and welcomed. Through interaction children can "pool" their interpretations, test out their predictions, and compare views. Through book discussions, literature and language games, activities, and partnership reading the children can work together to enrich their perceptions.

This enrichment expands as the children respond through art, drama, storytelling, writing, and one-to-one sharing. This is not meant to imply that verbalization and activity are the only indicators that children have had a rewarding experience with literature; they can appreciate in a quiet way, too.

Integration

Literature has relevance in an early childhood program because of its planned interdisciplinary base. One of the major objectives of an interdisciplinary approach is to help children better understand the world around them. Through this approach the classroom becomes a microcosm of a child's world. For example, animals, rocks, and flowers are displayed accompanying trade books that stimulate curiosity, questions, and understanding on these subjects. Folktales are used in a social studies unit, poetry patterns help children practice grammar, and quotations offer a model of oral discourse.

The Reading Corner

A special place to read—a reading corner—is an important part of the classroom environment. The area need not be elaborate; it *should* invite children to feel cozy and provide many materials for reading. Even children who are in a day-care center or nursery school need lots of exposure to books before they learn to read; they need books and related materials even more than older children who can read, for it is only through long and continued exposure to books that youngsters acquire the insatiable desire to learn to read and keep reading. Following general guidelines for the physical layout of the corner and for the acquisition and use of books will increase the popularity and effectiveness of this approach.

Layout

The reading corner should be in a quiet, well-lit part of the room where interference is at a minimum. Spaciousness—"psychological breathing room"—allows enough room for some children to group themselves for formal or informal activities and for others to read alone. A cheerful, colorful corner is more inviting than a dark, drab one.

One elementary classroom includes bean bag chairs to curl up in; another has a bright red bathtub filled with cushions for lounging and reading. A day-care center has an old rowboat for the children to climb into to look at books. A large appliance box with a lamp inside or a comfortable chair to curl up in provides a nice quiet space. A sofa can provide either space for quiet reading or discussions about books. Old sofas may look drab, but with ingenuity, attractive covers can be made. Centers for reading often have rocking chairs for adults to read to children, or child-sized ones for children to use for rocking and reading.

The corner can include bulletin boards and charts to invite reading. You might introduce an author through posters and display his or her books nearby. A poetry box could house copies of class favorites, and mobiles might display the report of someone's reading. The reading corner could have shelves, bulletin board space, dioramas, pictures, scripts, puppets, and realia that supplement stories or are part of the reports that a reader chooses to make in response to reading.

Place aids and visual equipment that encourage book sharing and storytelling close to the reading corner. Such items as feltboards and figures for arranging a story, puppets, roller boxes, picture stands, and realia can be motivation enough for reading and sharing.

Book Acquisition and Use

Whether the reading corner is a place for extended reading or a place to check out books with a simple card system, it is important to provide books that will satisfy the varied interests and reading levels of the children within the class. Books selected by the teacher should be combined with "my favorite story" that a student brings and adds to the corner for a short time. There should be magazines, newspapers, brochures, charts, and maps for reading as well. Student-authored books add a lot of interest, as do copies of a story recorded on a cassette by the young author.

You can begin a classroom library by borrowing from the school library, the public library or bookmobile, and your students. You might get donations from parent volunteers (who elicit donations), library rejects (making new covers isn't hard), children in your classroom, and bonus books from bookclubs (Scholastic, for example). Buy inexpensive used books at garage sales, auctions, library sales, bookstore sales, and bookclubs.

Children enjoy participating in money-raising activities to contribute to a classroom library collection. You might set up a policy stating that each child who contributes two books to the collection gets to keep one. At the end of the school year each child could take several books home to keep and read over the summer. If you do accept donations, be sure to check the contents and the quality of the books carefully. You don't want to include books that are likely to offend parents.

A loft with pillows, a fenced corral with saddles, a listening post with earphones. Wherever the area, whatever the furniture and format, the important thing is to allow *time* and *space* for exploring books.

Props, Puppets and Other Paraphernalia

One of the first ways young children make stories come alive is through props of one sort or another. The dressup corner turns into the setting of a story or puppets become story characters. Play that evolves from stories young children have heard or read occurs incidentally, but it can also be planned by the teacher.

Props

Children love props of all kinds. "Make-believe" can happen with a scarf, an umbrella, or an old pair of glasses. The props should be simple and classroom-made when possible. Often a hat, name tag, mask, shirt, or apron can be the springboard for story drama. A star on a stick for a fairy godmother or pinned on a shirt for a sheriff may enhance characterization.

You might collect props to favorite stories and store them in shopping bags or shoe boxes labeled with a picture on the front so the children can easily find them. When using props with young children, you might try "warm-ups." Use new and unusual activities to loosen up. For example, use props to pantomime "Jack Be Nimble," "Pickety Fence," "The Little Red Hen," or situations such as the sun coming up or feet being stuck in the mud. Use a scarf to pantomime a butterfly coming from a chrysalis. Pantomime "The Worm" (Roberts).

Stories Using Props

Many stories lend themselves to acting out with props. You might start with some classic favorites.

"Little Red Riding Hood" (de Regniers)
Materials needed: red cape with hood; pipe cleaner glasses for grandmother; mask or hood, and sock claws for wolf; cardboard axe for hunter. Children may not volunteer to be the wolf, so the teacher might take that role initially.

"The Three Bears" (Galdone)
Materials needed: bib for Baby Bear, skirt for Mama Bear, hat for Papa Bear, three bowls, three chairs, and six chairs or mats put together to form three beds. The story can be pantomimed as read or spontaneously dramatized.

"Stone Soup" (Brown)
Materials needed: large pot, large stone, long handled spoon, assorted vegetables, aprons for cooks, hats for travelers, three-cornered hats for soldiers. Dramatize the story as a narrator reads it. This is a particularly good story since each child can act as a village person. Soup can actually be made in class with each child bringing one vegetable to add to the pot.

For some stories a simple prop can accompany the reading of the story. An Indian blanket may be used to accompany the reading of "Annie and the Old One" (Miles) or "Wait for Me, Watch for Me, Eula Bee" (Beatty). A diary would add interest to "Harriet the Spy" (Fitzhugh). Here are some other simple prop ideas:

Rachel and Obadiah (Turkle): Paper towel roll as spyglass; two silver coins

Caps for Sale (Slobodkina): Caps (all colors and kinds)

Blueberries for Sal (McCloskey): Tin pails (or plastic buckets)

The Snowy Day (Keats): A large cotton ball

Cinderella (Perrault): A fancy lady's slipper

Carrot Seed (Krauss): An orange-painted paper sack with green yarn for the top

Sylvester and the Magic Pebble (Steig): Red pebble

Beast of Monsieur Racine (Ungerer): A blanket or large rug

Andy and the Lion (Daughtery): Small stick (toothpick)

Strega Nona (de Paola): Large pot and spoon

Shoemaker and the Elves (Grimm): Small hammers and slippers

Puppets

Children sometimes identify puppets with real life situations. Often a child who is too shy to dramatize in any other way will "act" behind a puppet. Children sometimes show more spontaneity and vocal expression when sharing ideas "through" a puppet. Puppet plays encourage group participation and cooperation because the success and fun of the drama are dependent on total team effort.

A literature-rich classroom environment will include permanent puppets that are virtually indestructible (such as paper mache or sewn hand puppets) as well as temporary puppets that will be used for a short time and for a limited purpose (such as paper bag and finger puppets). It will include puppets made specifically for one story (three bears and Goldilocks) as well as character puppets that might be used for several stories (a hen for *Rosie's Walk* or *The Little Red Hen*). Even puppets not specifically made to accompany stories enhance literature appreciation because children will naturally make up stories as they play with puppet characters. It is wise to remember when dealing with young children that monster puppets will elicit monster behaviors, puppets with fangs will often be violent, etc. Many fairy tales incorporate these negative character traits en route to overcoming evil with good. Put variety into the puppet characters you make, however.

Making puppets can be lots of fun. Even very young children can make their own puppets under certain conditions. If a specific pattern is to be followed, it is best if adults make the puppets. Puppet-making by children should be a creative, thoughtful experience, according to art educators. Children can be guided by questions like, "What shape are a bear's ears?" or "What could you use to make long, blond hair?", but they should not be asked to copy a model. Each child's puppet should be a unique creation. When children make the puppets they use, they usually grow more attached to the puppet character, thereby developing a deeper concept of characterization in a story.

Types of Puppets

There are numerous materials that can be used in puppet construction but basically there are four types suitable for young children:

1. *Puppets covering the hand or fingers.* These may be made by children from paper bags and cloth cut into body shapes (fig. 1). Adults can make sock and finger puppets for young children. A pattern for sock puppets suitable for *The Very Hungry Caterpillar* or *The Bremen-Town Musicians* is found in figure 2. Glove puppets and finger puppets can include tiny characters attached to each finger. For very young children one puppet on one finger is perfect because it requires little dexterity to manipulate. Try making "Two Little Blackbirds" out of paper, with tabs to fasten around the finger (fig. 3). Puppet patterns for *The Shoemaker and the Elves* are also given in figure 4.

2. *Puppets attached to sticks.* These are heads and bodies attached to tongue depressors, dowels, pencils, or clothespins. They may be used on a stage or as shadow puppets. A teacher might make a lamb (fig. 5) for *Mary Had a Little Lamb* and dress a clothespin (fig. 6) for Mary. Young children, however, can have lots of fun creating many different characters on construction paper or oaktag that can be made into puppets by attaching them to sticks. Small groups of children might work together to make the characters for several different stories.

3. *Puppets on strings.* The marionette is difficult for the beginning puppeteer, but children can soon learn to tilt the crossbar to which the arm and leg strings are attached for walking, jumping, and arm-rolling movements. Adults would need to make the puppets, which might be either animals or people. The person in figure 7 might be the man in *Too Much Noise.*

4. *Puppets from odds and ends.* Almost anything can be used to make a puppet. If teacher and students collect things like boxes, cans, egg cartons, styrofoam, buttons, and popsicle sticks, and have a scrap box for fabric, yarn, fringe, ricrac, etc., the children will need very little coaxing to make creative puppets on their own. You, too, can think of ideas. One teacher's favorite is a "craggy lion" made from a vegetable brush.

The keys to using puppets successfully in a literature program are never to criticize the creative efforts of young children and to be able to spot easily stories that naturally lend themselves to puppetry.

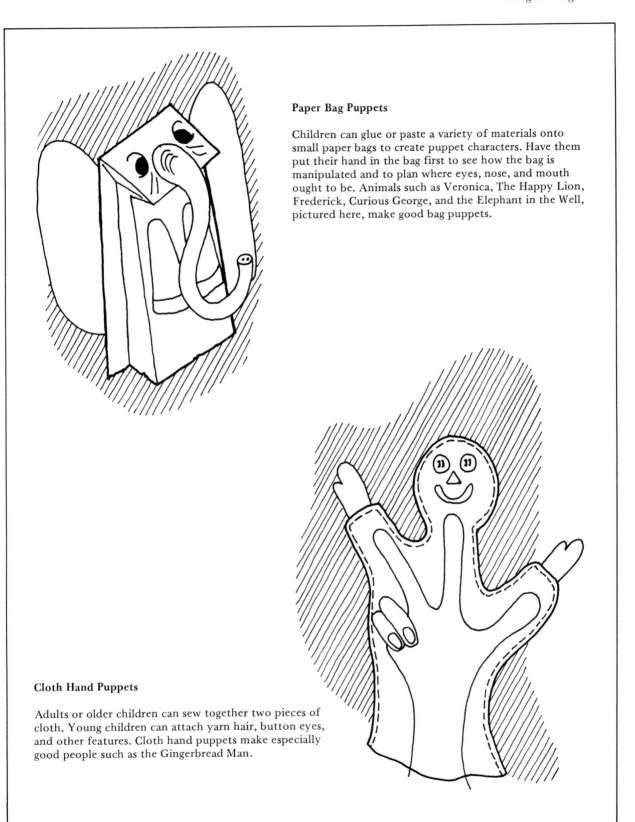

Paper Bag Puppets

Children can glue or paste a variety of materials onto small paper bags to create puppet characters. Have them put their hand in the bag first to see how the bag is manipulated and to plan where eyes, nose, and mouth ought to be. Animals such as Veronica, The Happy Lion, Frederick, Curious George, and the Elephant in the Well, pictured here, make good bag puppets.

Cloth Hand Puppets

Adults or older children can sew together two pieces of cloth. Young children can attach yarn hair, button eyes, and other features. Cloth hand puppets make especially good people such as the Gingerbread Man.

Figure 1. Paper bag puppets and cloth hand puppets.

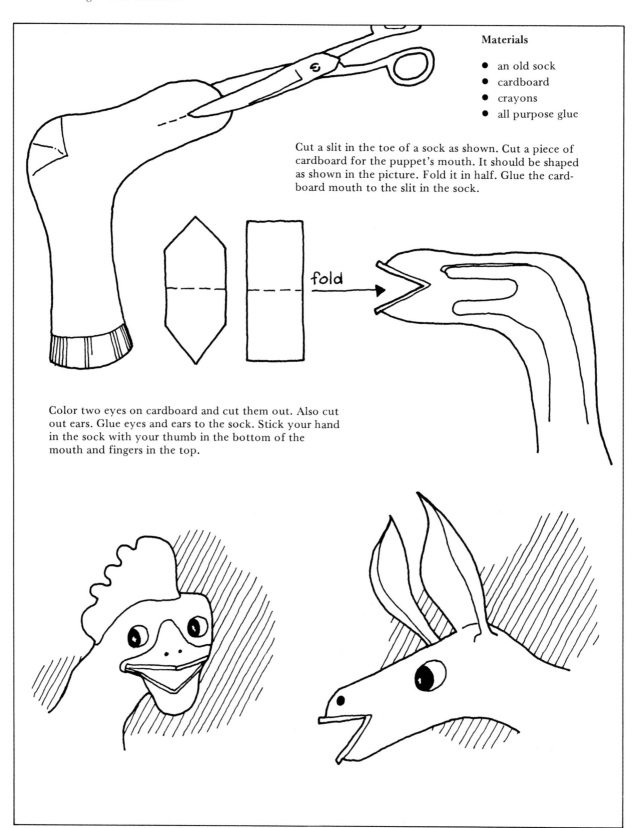

Materials

- an old sock
- cardboard
- crayons
- all purpose glue

Cut a slit in the toe of a sock as shown. Cut a piece of cardboard for the puppet's mouth. It should be shaped as shown in the picture. Fold it in half. Glue the cardboard mouth to the slit in the sock.

fold

Color two eyes on cardboard and cut them out. Also cut out ears. Glue eyes and ears to the sock. Stick your hand in the sock with your thumb in the bottom of the mouth and fingers in the top.

Figure 2. Sock puppets.

Cut two patterns out of black construction paper.
Scotch tape tabs together.
Children use one on each hand.

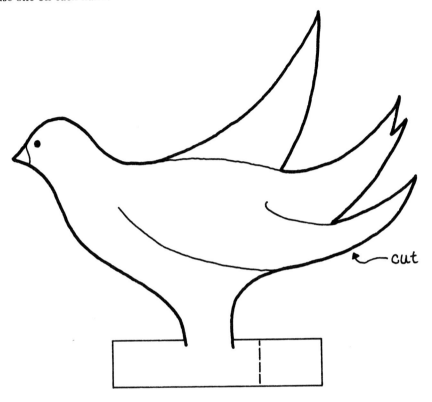

cut

Poem	Finger Movements
Two little blackbirds sitting on a hill	Show puppets in front
One named Jack	move one
One named Jill	move the other
Fly away Jack	move Jack behind back
Fly away Jill	move Jill behind back
Come back Jack	bring Jack back out front
Come back Jill	bring Jill back out front

Figure 3. Pattern for "Two Little Blackbirds" finger puppet.

Make out of construction paper or soft cardboard.
You might color the original elves shabbily and make
extra jackets with tabs to attach at the end of the story.

Figure 4. Finger puppet patterns for "The Elves and the Shoemaker."

Trace the pattern of the body, tail, legs, and ears of the
lamb onto white cardboard or heavy construction paper.

Cut out the parts and fit the grooves together, as shown,
to make the lamb. Glue a stick to the body, as shown, so
that you can manipulate it while you are out of sight
behind a table or stage floor. You may want to glue
cotton all over it to make a woolly lamb.

Figure 5. Stick puppet pattern for Mary's lamb.

Clothes pin

Front of coat of blue construction paper

Coat back

cut patterns

Hat with feather

Skirt—to be lapped at dotted line and pasted together

Color with marker

Figure 6. Clothes pin puppet pattern for Mary.

A string puppet may be made from heavy cut-outs with string hinges. The figure is moved with a rod attached to arms and head.

Another method would be to attach strings to head and arms of a stuffed animal or rag doll with a control rod for manipulation.

Figure 7. Simple string puppet.

Stories for Use with Puppets

Puppets can be made to fit a specific story, or new stories can be written to include a puppet someone has created. For example, one may decide to tell "The Little Red Hen" and then select the characters necessary: the hen, the pig, the dog, etc. Or the furry caterpillar puppet Joshua made might inspire a "Monarch in the Spring" story that could be dramatized.

Short stories with a lot of action, repetition, and simple settings make appropriate beginning projects for puppet plays. The story that is spontaneous with little or no memorization is usually the most successful. The following stories are especially adaptable for puppetry:

"The Gingerbread Boy" (Galdone)

"The Cock, the Mouse, and the Little Red Hen" (traditional folktale)

"Bedtime for Frances" (Hoban)

"Henny-Penny" (traditional folktale)

"Good Night, Owl!" (Hutchins)

"The Mitten" (Tresselt)

"Tale of Peter Rabbit" (Potter)

"The Three Billy Goats Gruff" (Asbjornsen and Mae)

"The Town Mouse and the Country Mouse" (Aesop)

Puppet stages may or may not be needed for the storytelling. Sometimes a single puppet seated on a lap is all that is required. At other times a table turned on its side makes a stage ready to hide puppeteers. You might also try cutting a stage out of an appliance box (see figure 8). An excellent project for a parent with carpentry skills or for some older children is the making of a permanent stage. You will find that a stage in your classroom virtually assures that youngsters will play with puppets.

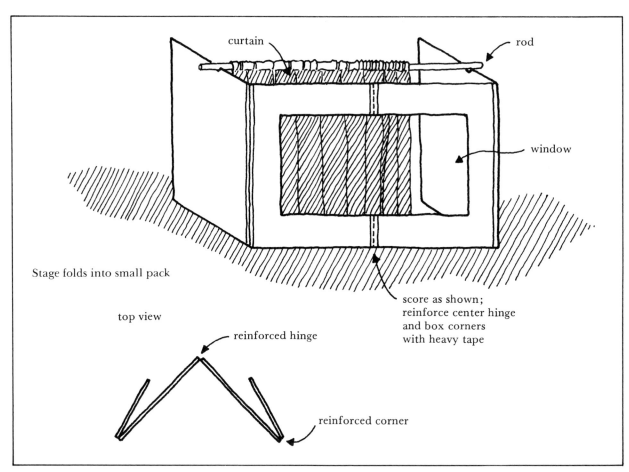

Figure 8. Puppet stage from appliance box.

Activities with Puppets

1. "Where the Wild Things Are" (Sendak)

   Materials needed: "Max" puppet; unlimited number of Wild Things puppets; three backdrops—the bedroom, the boat and water, and the home of the Wild Things. Children can act out their own parts; the Wild Things (one on each hand) can be accompanied by music that the children select as "wild rumpus music."

2. "The Three Little Pigs" (Galdone)

   Materials needed: Finger puppets of three pigs, wolf, and a backdrop for each house. This story is so well known that children will spontaneously act it out. Again, background music would be fun to record and intersperse at climactic spots.

3. "The Three Billy Goats Gruff" (Asbjornsen and Mae)

   Materials needed: Outline of bridge, shadow puppets for three goats (varying sizes) and a troll, bedsheet hung high enough for the puppeteers to stand behind and a projector or lamp behind them. (See figure 9 for a sketch showing how to use shadow puppets.) Experimenting is necessary to get the right size and placement of characters for a shadow play. A narrator reading the story can leave the actors free to move with precision.

Suggested Reading: Puppetry

Baird, Bill. *The Art of the Puppet.* New York: Plays, Inc., 1966.

Binyon, Helen. *Puppetry Today.* New York: Watson-Guptill Publications, Inc., 1966.

Boylan, Eleanor. *How to be a Puppeteer.* New York: E. P. Dutton, 1970.

Bursill, Henry. *Hand Shadows to be Thrown upon a Wall.* New York: Dover Publications, Inc., 1967.

Chernoff, G. T. *Puppet Party.* New York: Walker & Co., 1971.

Cochrane, Louise. *Shadow Puppets in Color.* New York: Plays, Inc., 1972.

Currell, David. *The Complete Book of Puppetry.* New York: Plays, Inc., 1975.

Hooper, Grizella. *Puppet Making through the Grades.* Worcester, Mass.: Davis Publications, Inc., 1966.

Jackson, Sheila. *Simple Puppetry.* New York: Watson-Guptill Publications, Inc., 1969.

Kampmann, Lothar. *Creating with Puppets.* New York: Plays, Inc., 1980.

Miller, Donna. *Egg Carton Critters.* New York: Scholastic Book Services, 1979.

Mulholland, John. *Practical Puppetry.* Austin, Texas: Jenkins Publishing Co., 1961.

Philpott, A. R. *Let's Make Puppets.* New York: D. Van Nostrand Co., 1972.

Richter, Dorothy. *Fell's Guide to Hand Puppets: How to Make and Use Them.* New York: Frederick Fell Publishers, Inc., 1970.

Ross, Laura. *Finger Puppets: Easy to Make, Fun to Use.* New York: Lothrop, Lee & Shepard Books, 1971.

Ross, Laura. *Hand Puppets: How to Make and Use Them.* New York: Lothrop, Lee & Shepard Books, 1969.

Scott, Louise Binder, et al. *Puppets for All Grades.* Dansville, N.Y.: F. A. Owen, 1970.

Children's Book References

Aesop. *The Town Mouse and the Country Mouse.* Illus. Boris Artzybasheff. New York: Viking Press, 1932.

Asbjornsen, P. C., and Mae, J. E. *The Three Billy Goats Gruff.* New York: Harcourt Brace Jovanovich, Inc., 1957.

Beatty, Patricia. *Wait for Me, Watch for Me, Eula Bee.* New York: William Morrow Co., Inc., 1978.

Bishop, Claire. *The Five Chinese Brothers.* New York: Coward, McCann & Geoghegan, Inc., 1938.

Brown, Marcia. *Stone Soup.* New York: Charles Scribner's Sons, 1947.

Carle, Eric. *The Very Hungry Caterpillar.* New York: Collins-World, 1972.

Daughtery, James. *Andy and the Lion.* New York: Viking Press, 1938.

de Paola, Tomie. *Strega Nona.* Englewood Cliffs, N.J.: Prentice-Hall, Inc., 1975.

de Regniers, Beatrice S. *The Little Red Hen.* New York: Atheneum Publishers, 1972.

de Regniers, Beatrice S. *Red Riding Hood.* New York: Atheneum Publishers, 1972.

Fitzhugh, Louise. *Harriet the Spy.* New York: Harper & Row, Publishers, Inc., 1964.

Galdone, Paul. *The Gingerbread Boy.* New York: Seabury Press, Inc., 1975.

Galdone, Paul. *The Little Red Hen.* New York: Seabury Press, Inc., 1973.

Galdone, Paul. *The Three Bears.* New York: Seabury Press, Inc., 1972.

Galdone, Paul. *Three Little Pigs.* New York: Seabury Press, Inc., 1970.

Grimm Brothers. *Shoemaker and the Elves.* Illus. A. Adams. New York: Charles Scribner's Sons, 1960.

Gross, Ruth B. *The Bremen-Town Musicians.* Illus. Jack Kent. New York: Scholastic Book Services, 1975.

"Henny Penny." In *Comparative Anthology of Children's Literature,* edited by Mary Ann Nelson. New York: Holt, Rinehart and Winston, Inc., 1972.

Figure 9. Shadow puppets for "The Three Billy Goats Gruff."

Hoban, Russell. *Bedtime for Frances.* New York: Harper & Row, Publishers, Inc., 1960.

Hutchins, Pat. *Good-Night Owl!* New York: Macmillan Publishing Co., Inc., 1972.

Hutchins, Pat. *Rosie's Walk.* New York: Macmillan Publishing Co., Inc., 1968.

"Jack Be Nimble." In *Comparative Anthology of Children's Literature,* edited by Mary Ann Nelson. New York: Holt, Rinehart and Winston, Inc., 1972.

Keats, Ezra Jack. *The Snowy Day.* New York: Viking Press, 1962.

Krauss, Ruth. *The Carrot Seed.* New York: Harper & Row, Publishers, Inc., 1945.

McCloskey, Robert. *Blueberries for Sal.* New York: Viking Press, 1948.

McCord, David. "The Pickety Fence." In *Comparative Anthology of Children's Literature,* edited by Mary Ann Nelson. New York: Holt, Rinehart and Winston, Inc., 1972.

McGovern, Ann. *Too Much Noise.* Illus. Simms Taback. Boston: Houghton Mifflin Co., 1967.

Miles, M. *Annie and the Old One.* Boston, Mass.: Little, Brown & Co., 1971.

Perrault, C. *Cinderella.* New York: Thomas Y. Crowell Co., 1978.

Potter, Beatrix. *Tale of Peter Rabbit.* New York: Frederick Warne & Co., Inc., 1902.

Roberts, Elizabeth M. "The Worm." In *A Book of Children's Literature,* edited by Lillian Hollowell. New York: Holt, Rinehart and Winston, Inc., 1966.

Sendak, Maurice. *Where the Wild Things Are.* New York: Harper & Row, Publishers, Inc., 1963.

Slobodkina, Esphyr. *Caps for Sale.* Glenview, Ill.: Addison-Wesley Publishing Co., Inc., 1947.

Steig, William. *Sylvester and the Magic Pebble.* New York: E. P. Dutton, 1973.

Tresselt, Alvin. *The Mitten.* New York: Lothrop, Lee & Shepard Books, 1964.

Turkle, Brinton. *Rachel and Obadiah.* New York: E. P. Dutton, 1978.

Ungerer, Tomi. *The Beast of Monsieur Racine.* New York: Farrar, Straus & Giroux, Inc., 1971.

3 STORYTELLING TECHNIQUES

Marilou Sorenson
University of Utah

Once the classroom environment has been designed to provide many opportunities for involving children with literature, you will want to develop your skills and expand your repertoire of ideas. You'll want to be able to tell stories with and without props, to help children dramatize stories and chant rhymes and refrains, and to incorporate many strategies for helping children develop the literature habit into their daily and weekly routines.

Storytelling

For lo, the storyteller comes.
Let fall the trumpets; hush the drums . . . .

Storytelling is an old but neglected art. When modeled by the teacher, the children soon learn the joy of watching a storyteller. One little boy said, "Teacher, do it again, so that I can see your eyes tell it!" What he really was asking was to see the expression of the full face while it was told and not just her glance as the story was read.

Skill in storytelling comes through thoughtful story selection and careful preparation. The story should be one that suits the audience as well as the teller. As one reads a selection the following should be considered:

Is the story one that is appropriate for telling, or should it be read?

Is the story appropriate for the group or groups for which it is intended?

Is the story appropriate for the setting in which it will be told?

Are the mood and style suitable in terms of the storyteller's personality?

Does the story still "click" after several readings or is it boring?

There are five basic steps to preparing a story for storytelling:

1. *Knowing the story.* You must know the story so well that it is a part of you. The characters will become your friends and the story setting will be pictured in your mind. The scenes or story situations will begin to follow in order and the mood and style will be felt throughout the preparation. Of course, one way to really get to know a story is to read it aloud repeatedly.

2. *Analyzing the story.* As the story is read, these points should be considered in an analysis of the story: Is the story appropriate for the listener, the storyteller, and the occasion? Can it or should it be adapted for the storyteller's personality? Where could it be cut or elaborated? What effects will be used, such as narration, songs, realia, gestures, speaking voices? Does the story "live" enough (is there enough action) for telling and retelling? Has it been told for long enough to be called a classic, or will it become one?

3. *Reading and rereading.* Read and reread the story until it is fixed in your mind, know the plot, characterization, and sequence of events. Leave the story for a day. At the end of that time check yourself to see what you remember. Consider which of the author's phrases and words you have retained.

4. *Making cue cards.* Reread the story again. Underline certain words, events, or points for review. Make a cue card as an abstract of the story structure, or use an outline format. An example of a familiar story is given in figure 10.

Title: "Three Little Pigs"
Source: *A Comparative Anthology of Children's Literature*, Nelson, p. 419.
Telling Time: 8 minutes
Three pigs—left home to seek fortune
One: House of straw
    wolf destroys—pig runs away
Two: House of sticks
    wolf destroys—pig goes to brother
Three: House of bricks
    wolf and pig to apple tree
    wolf and pig to fair
    wolf is killed
Resolution: The three pigs live in the brick house together.
Comments: Could be used for dramatization. Could use pictures.

Figure 10. Cue card for "The Three Little Pigs."

5. *Story review and rehearsal.* When you know the story thoroughly, rehearse orally. Only through review and practice can a storyteller be effective. Rehearsal does not imply memorization of the story. Memorizing word-by-word involves an exorbitant amount of time. When the story is committed to memory, the spontaneity of the story may be lost, for the storyteller might concentrate more on the exactness of the words than on expression, listener feedback, and personal enjoyment. Too, what can a storyteller do if the memorized text is forgotten? There is no extemporaneous "comeback" when something is learned verbatim. An exception to the "don't memorize" rule would be to master a refrain in the story.

This phrase from *Millions of Cats* by Wanda Gág is necessary to make the story live:

Hundreds of cats
Thousands of cats
Millions and billions and trillions of cats.

or this one from "Gingerbread Boy":

I've run away from a little old woman
A little old man
A barn full of threshers
A field full of mowers
A cow
A pig
And I can run away from you, I can, I can.

or

Run, run as fast as you can.
You can't catch me,
I'm the gingerbread man!

Time the rehearsal. If the story is too lengthy, consider the points that can be cut without loss of story impact; for example, the gingerbread boy could run away from only three "chasers" instead of four.

Practice telling the story into a recorder in front of a mirror. Play back the tape. Listen and look for those qualities that you wish to continue. Consider ways of substituting for those defects that need to be discarded. Listen for sentences that run together. Use pauses to give greater impact. Note posture and gestures as they set and maintain a definite mood during the storytelling session.

Now you are ready for an audience. You might begin by telling the story to only one child or a small group as a transition to group storytelling. The story is told directly and sincerely, freely using the face, arms, and body to add interest, though you must be sure that motions do not distract from the story. These body movements should be your natural expressions; they are not contrived nor are they meant to be a dramatization. As you advance in your storytelling ability, you will find that you do not need gestures. Your voice alone will carry the story.

The basic mediums that you will use in storytelling are the language and the voice. Some teachers can use dialogue, varied expression and inflection well; others prefer a simple narrative. The voice can indicate many moods and changes in character. Begin with a hushed voice; then change volume as the story changes. These changes in voice can supplement an otherwise ordinary presentation.

The element of suspense and surprise is established by what Briggs and Wagner (1970) call "the pause that entrances." A pause after a statement gives emphasis to facts, allows the listener to adjust to change in plot, and builds anticipation. The storyteller can gauge audience reaction during the pause and prepare for impact. A pause that may seem endless to a teller is only a flashing moment to a listener. Yet it is a form of relief from a constant barrage of words and feelings to both teller and listener. Pausing is a technique that warrants practice and use.

An effective storyteller controls the rate from the beginning of the session. The younger the audience, the more the storyteller needs to determine whether the speed is appropriate. When children get restless, speed up, skip parts, and dramatize a bit more. The type of story, also, helps determine the rate of the telling. A tale of humor can proceed at a more lilting pace than a story of pathos.

The introduction should be delivered more slowly than any other part of the story. Often, in a rush to get to the heart of the tale, or because of nervousness, this is not done. The information found in the introduction of children's stories is basic to the entire story and should not be rushed.

The conclusion is presented at a slower rate than the body of the story. The story will have more impact and leave a lasting impression upon the children if you slow down at the end.

If the exact language of the book is important, such as dialects and colorful language, the books should be read aloud or more preparation time is needed. Examples of books with rich language for reading are those of Dr. Seuss, Kipling, and Uncle Remus. Also, just as books with rich language should be read, so should illustrations be shared. The illustrations in "Finders Keepers," for example, add to the story line and should be shared as the story is read; children should be able to see the elephant as he sits on the nest in Dr. Seuss's "Horton Hatches the Egg."

Storytelling Aids

Storytelling can be varied using aids such as roller stories and feltboards. With a roller box the pictures are drawn by the children and pasted on a long roll of shelf paper (fig. 11). Narration can accompany the pictures in the form of captions, spoken narration, or a tape recording.

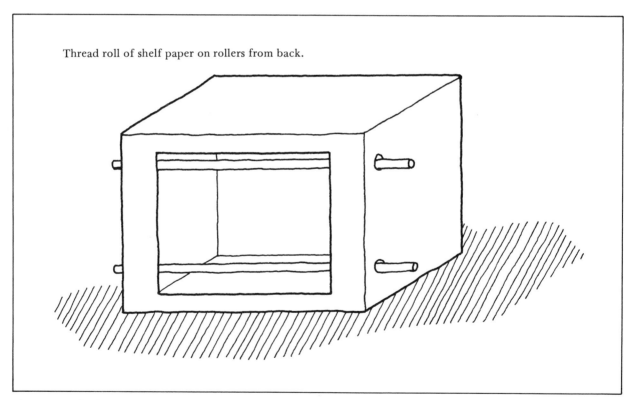

Thread roll of shelf paper on rollers from back.

Figure 11. Roller box.

Flannelboards, also called feltboards, can be easily constructed by stapling flannel or felt to a piece of heavy cardboard, triwall, or plywood. Triwall makes an especially light, portable flannelboard. If you make the board in three parts with hinges, it can be folded for storage and can support itself. But a flat board leaning against a wall works just fine, also.

Characters and scenery can be made from flannel, felt, heavy pellon, or oaktag. You can trace characters directly from a book onto pellon, but very little children sometimes have difficulty manipulating flimsy cloth pieces; oaktag is sturdier. Use carbon paper to trace characters onto the oaktag and then color them. Covering oaktag with contact paper or laminating the pieces makes them last longer. Glue heavy grade sandpaper or velcro on the backs of pieces to make them stick to the flannel. Brush the flannel if it becomes flat with use and pieces don't stick well.

When introducing a flannelboard story to a class, the teacher usually tells the story and moves the pieces the first time. The second time children may want to take turns moving pieces while the teacher tells the story. If it is a familiar story, the children can tell it independently.

Store all the pieces for each story in large envelopes or manila folders in a box right next to the flannelboard so the pieces don't get lost. Label envelopes with pictures and note the number of characters or flannel pieces. You might also tape-record the story (particularly if it is less well known) and leave the tape recorder next to the flannelboard where individuals or small groups of children can play the tape as they manipulate the pieces.

Stories suitable for flannelboards are similar to those suitable for puppetry except that there can be more characters, and pieces don't have to be story characters. For example, *Caps for Sale* would be difficult to do with puppets, but is a good flannelboard tale because groups of hats can be individual pieces. Cumulative stories and songs that keep adding pieces (*The Farmer in the Dell, I Had a Rooster, Ask Mr. Bear,* and *Brown Bear, Brown Bear, What Do You See?*, for example) are excellent flannelboard tales.

Participation Stories and Choral Speaking

In participation stories, the storyteller develops the thought of the story or selection and the audience participates by repeating a refrain, adding bodily action, or representing a small character part. In choral speaking, all children participate, some in the entire selection, others as solo parts and voices. Both types of participation add variety to a storytelling session. The first, the participation story, requires less preparation and is actually a simple form of choral speaking. It can be used with very young children but it is enjoyed by adults as well.

Participation Stories

The success of participation stories depends on the active participation of everyone in the group. For the young child three or four cues can be remembered. Older children can learn more responses. "Trying out" parts before they are read together is a good idea. A teacher may say, "This row will be ducks. Let me hear what all the ducks will say when it is your turn," or "When I say run, run, run, what action will you do?" or "On which word do we all stand up?"

Participation stories can be adapted from familiar folktales or any story that allows for actions or sounds to be interjected. The following are versions of two types: sound stories and action stories or poems.

Little Duck
(Sound Story)

(This is a story game for everyone to play. One player reads the story aloud. Then each player takes the part of an animal. The players give their sound effects whenever their names are mentioned.)

cow—moo, moo	cat—meow, meow
horse—neigh, neigh	duck—quack, quack
pig—oink, oink	mouse—squeak, squeak
dog—bow-wow	rooster—cock-a-doodle-doo

The animals on Oak Hill Farm were noisy one morning. The rooster (cock-a-doodle-doo) was crowing. The cow (moo, moo) was mooing. The dog (bow-wow) was barking, and the cat (meow, meow) was meowing. Everybody was looking for little duck (quack, quack). Little duck (quack, quack) was gone. The cow (moo, moo) looked all through the sweet clover in the pasture. But no little duck (quack, quack). The horse (neigh, neigh) galloped into the next field. But no little duck (quack, quack). The fat, fat pig (oink, oink) pushed all the mud out of his puddle. But he could not find little duck (quack, quack).

Then the animals hurried down to the pond once more to look for little duck (quack, quack). They all called him. (Everybody shouts.) But no little duck (quack, quack). The animals were quiet as they walked back to the barn. They had looked everywhere, but could not find little duck (quack, quack).

Suddenly, a little mouse (squeak, squeak) came scurrying out the barn. How he squeaked! He led the animals back into the barn and over to his nest in a quiet corner. And there was little duck (quack, quack) asleep on the mouse's (squeak, squeak) nest. What a shout the animals gave! (Everybody shouts.) They had found little duck (quack, quack). They woke him up with their shouting. Little duck (quack, quack) was rushed back to the duck pond, where, after all, little ducks (quack, quack) belong.

Let's Pretend
(Action Poem)

(Before you read a verse, ask a child how to make the motion that the verse suggests, such as "How do you ride a pony?" Ask the child how the pony would fall. Emphasize the fact that the child must stop at the end of each verse. Student names may be substituted.)

Oh, let's pretend! Yes, let's pretend
That we are something new.
Let's pretend we're lots of things
And see what we can do.

David is a cowboy
Riding up a hill,
  (Ride pony)
Until his pony stumbles
And David takes a spill.
  (Fall down)

Jeannie is an autumn leaf,
She twirls and twirls around.
  (Dance with many turns)
She twists and turns and twirls again,
And tumbles to the ground.
  (Bend way over)

Kevin is an airplane
Flying high and grand,
  (Extend arms and glide around room)
Until he sees an airport
Where he has to land.
  (Bend knees until extended arms touch floor)

Sally is a firefly,
Flitting in the night;
  (Dance with jerky motions)
Until the morning comes
And she puts out her light.
  (Kneel down and curl up)

Kenny is a snowman
Who smiles and looks around.
  (Stand still and smile)

Until the Sun smiles back at him
And he melts to the ground.
  (Gradually kneels as if melting)

What else can you pretend?
What do other people do?
If you will act it out,
I'll try to do it, too.

    Bernice Wells Carlson
    Listen & Help Tell the Story. New York: Abingdon
    Press, 1965.

Choral Speaking

Choral speaking is one way of using literature in a group setting. Songs, poetry, and nursery rhymes are sources for choral speaking. You might make a chart or ditto of the selection so all can "read" it together. Rebus (picture writing) can be used for nonreaders. Make markings of words for emphasis, solo parts, and sound effects. Encourage the group to decide the parts, pauses, inflections, and levels of projection. It is important to practice and refine the choral speaking before performing it for others.

Do:

1. Know the selection well.
2. Read the poem aloud to the class with a sense of rhythm and sound pattern.
3. Look for possibilities of contrast (high/low, fast/slow, question/answer, echo) and balance within the poem.
4. Read the poem a second time aloud to the class.
5. Invite the class to participate.
6. Keep the voices soft. Volume can be increased after the tonal patterns are accurate.
7. Repeat the poem together.

Don't:

1. Don't choose material beyond the children's ability for enjoyment and appreciation.
2. Don't choose "star" pupils for all the solo parts. Leadership may be developed by giving the part to a child who can grow into it.
3. Don't use choral speaking as a "theatrical performance."

The following are examples of selections that lend themselves to choral speaking with suggestions for reciting them:

Animal Voices (one line per child)

"Bow-wow,"
    Says the dog;
"Mew, Mew,"
    Says the cat;
"Grunt, grunt,"
    Says the hog;
And, "Squeak,"
    Goes the rat.
"Tu-whu,"
    Says the owl.
"Caw-caw,"
    Says the crow;
"Quack, quack,"
    Says the duck;
And what cuckoos
    Say, you know! (all)

Echo

Solo 1
I sometimes wonder where he lives,
All
This Echo that I never see.
Girls
I hear his voice now in the hedge,
Boys
Then down behind the willow tree.

All   *Solo 2*
And when I call, "Oh, please come out,"
Solo 3   *All*
"Come out," he always quick replies.
Solo 2   *All*
"Hello, hello," again I say;
Solo 3   *Girls*
"Hello, hello," he softly cries.

All
He must be jolly, Echo must,
Boys
For when I laugh, "Ho, ho, ho, ho,"
Like any other friendly boy,
                Girls
He answers me with "Ho, ho, ho."

Solo 4
I think perhaps he'd like to play;
I know some splendid things to do.
All
He must be lonely hiding there;
Solo 5   *All*
I wouldn't like it. Now, would you?

The Chickens

Girls
Said the first little chicken,
With a queer little squirm,
Solo 1
"I wish I could find
A fat little worm."

Boys
Said the next little chicken,
With an odd little shrug:
Solo 2
"I wish I could find
A fat little bug."

Girls
Said a third little chicken,
With a small sigh of grief:
Solo 3
"I wish I could find
A green little leaf!"

Boys
Said the fourth little chicken,
With a faint little moan:
Solo 4
"I wish I could find
A wee gravel stone."

Solo 5   *Girls*
"Now, see here!" said the mother,
From the green garden patch,
Solo 5
"If you want any breakfast,
All
Just come here and scratch!"

Christmas Eve

Group 1: Tick Tock, Tick Tock (repeated as background for:)
Group 2: The clock ticks slowly, slowly in the hall
            And slower and slower the long hours crawl.
                It seems as though today
                Will never pass away
            The clock ticks slowly, s l o w l y in the hall.
Group 1: Tick Tock, Tick Tock, Tick (slowly)

Little Brown Rabbit

Teacher: Little brown rabbit went hoppity-hop
Class: Hoppity-hop, hoppity-hop!
Teacher: Into a garden without any stop,
Class: Hoppity-hop, hoppity-hop!
Teacher: He ate for his supper a fresh carrot top,
Class: Hoppity-hop, hoppity-hop!

Teacher: Then home went the rabbit without any stop,
Class: Hoppity-hop, hoppity-hop!

Other books that could be chanted include:

This Is the House That Jack Built (add each group as the tale progresses)

'Let's Marry!' Said the Cherry, by N. M. Bodecker

Drummer Hoff, adapted by Barbara Emberley

Over in the Meadow, by Ezra Jack Keats

Bill Martin's Instant Readers

Developing the Literature Habit

The most important element in the classroom is the enthusiastic teacher who allows time and opportunity for sharing literature. Preschool children and primary children learn to "read" pictures and interpret them. As children begin to match symbol and sound, they need time to practice sorting through the cues that help them recognize and identify the meaning of the printed page. Older, more proficient readers need to read to themselves, to internalize what is read, and to practice skills.

S.S.R.

S.S.R., Sustained Silent Reading (sometimes called U.S.S.R.—Uninterrupted Sustained Silent Reading), developed by Lyman Hunt, is one way to provide for this reading practice needed at all levels. During S.S.R. time, emphasis is placed upon practicing reading skills (or prereading skills) by reading or looking at books that children choose themselves. The teacher reads at this time also, providing a model for the children. There are no assignments or evaluative questions. The only requirement is that the time allotted be kept quiet and the reading practice (reading pictures for younger students) is respected. S.S.R. puts recreational reading into the curriculum alongside basic skills instruction. It not only enhances skill development by giving children practice, it also fosters enjoyment of literature.

In one first grade classroom S.S.R. was begun with an allotted time of three minutes. Within a few weeks the time had progressed to twenty minutes, followed by groans and sighs of regret when the timer signaled that time was up. In a day-care center, S.S.R. occurs just prior to nap time. Each child takes two or three books to the cot to look at before resting.

We believe that reading aloud daily to the class, to small groups within the class, and to individual children is so important that we have devoted all of chapter 4 to this topic.

The Library/Media Center Routine

When children and books get together early in life, reading is bound to happen. The earlier the habit of library use is begun with a child, the better the chance that the child will become hooked on visiting the library. Research shows that those students most successful in secondary and higher education were those students who were library users as very young children.

Visiting the school library/media center does many things for young children, in addition to helping them acquire library habits. Visits expose children to a much wider variety of literature in many media than would be available in a classroom. Although the environment may at first be overwhelming, with the help of the media specialist, children will soon feel at home in the library.

When the classroom teacher and librarian/media specialist work together as a team, the school library experience is likely to have optimal results. This relationship requires open communi-

---

MEMO TO: Sally Smith, Librarian/Media Specialist

FROM: Shirly Leveant [first grade teacher]

ABOUT: Reading levels and interests of children in my classroom

If the children in my classroom ask you to help them in book selection, here are their approximate reading levels (for books they could read by themselves) and some of their interests.

Child	*Reading level and Interests*
Sarah Albins	nonreader—dolls, dressups, clothes, jogging
Mike Bradshaw	2—sports, animals
Alicia Cramstoun	1.5—horses
Mark Cutter	1.0—boats, waterskiing
Laurel Lamme	1.5—gymnastics, ballet, music

Figure 12. Memo to librarian concerning student's reading levels and interests.

cation from one individual to the other. Classroom teachers need to be sure that librarians have information such as children's reading levels and interests so they can recommend books to individuals (fig. 12). Librarians can be tremendously helpful in suggesting books and other media resources to accompany thematic units of study.

Young children need time to explore the media center freely, to browse or read. Both in the classroom and in the library, adults must act as models by handling books gently and returning them promptly. Children should be encouraged to check books out, for it is only through repeated exposure to the same book that a "sense of story" develops. Libraries that require young children to be able to sign their names on tiny cards before they are permitted to check out books are depriving young children of books at the time when they most need them.

Library/media centers that are personalized with homemade materials are especially inviting. One kindergarten teacher takes a picture of each child in her class doing something special during the year. She writes a brief description, mounts the picture on oaktag, binds the pages into a book, and laminates them. At the end of each year she places the books in the school media center where they are enjoyed for years after as the children grow older. Another class makes books for the library by dictating stories to illustrations they have drawn.

Librarians and teachers can work together to plan special events for special times, such as National Book Week (fall), Library Week (spring), and observances unique to the locale. You could create your own special event by inviting local authors or illustrators to talk about their books, having parents share their hobbies accompanied by book displays on the same topic, or by having special showings of movies or filmstrips related to literature.

The teacher's attitude can play an important role in determining the impact of the school library/media center upon the young children in the class. Do you consider library time as important as time spent on basic skills such as reading and math? If so, there will be regularly scheduled library times that don't get missed for anything short of an emergency. It is also helpful if you and the librarian can schedule some "open" times when children can choose to go to the media center on their own. Eventually library use will be

a free choice of the individual, so it is important that during school hours children be given the opportunity to choose to use the library.

A Classroom Literature Routine Inventory

Figure 13 can help establish where you stand as an early childhood teacher in providing a regular classroom routine for involving your students with literature. Give yourself two points for every "yes" response, one point for every "sometimes" response, and no points for a "no" response.

Classroom Routine	Yes	Some-times	No
Do you regularly provide for:			
a. Sustained silent reading?			
b. Lap reading for each child? (having an adult or older child read to an individual child)			
c. Group story reading?			
d. Group storytelling?			
e. Using books related to topics of study?			
f. Children to dictate stories for you to write down?			
g. Visits to a school library/media center?			
h. Visits to a public library?			
i. Children to share literature?			
j. Invitations to resource people to visit your classroom?			
k. Choral speaking and participation activities?			

Figure 13. A classroom literature routine inventory.

The Community Library

It is more important to cultivate the public library habit than the school library habit, for the former can become a lifelong habit. Children enjoy field trips outside of school. If the public library or bookmobile is close enough, they would enjoy visiting it regularly. Parents need to be encouraged to establish a library routine for their families.

The public librarian may read aloud to the group or to individuals. There may be book displays, puppet shows, or other activities that entice young children to read and look at books. One public library scheduled a librarian to visit each day-care center in the community for an eight-week period. Once a week the librarian visited the center for a story hour. A large box of books was loaned to the center for the eight-week period. As a part of the program the librarian also conducted a meeting for the parents and staff of the center.

Public librarians are great resources for teachers who want to find books, media, references, book lists, and equipment. The public library in your community should definitely not be overlooked as you plan your literature curriculum.

Suggested Reading: Storytelling

Baker, Augusta, and Greene, Ellin. *Storytelling: Art and Technique.* New York: R. R. Bowker, Co., 1977.

Bauer, Caroline. *Handbook for Storytellers.* Chicago: American Library Association, 1977.

Briggs, Nancy E., and Wagner, Joseph A. *Children's Literature through Storytelling and Drama.* 2d. ed. Dubuque, Iowa: William C. Brown Co., Publishers, 1979.

Cathon, Laura, et al., eds. *Stories to Tell to Children: A Selected List.* Pittsburgh: University of Pittsburgh Press, 1974.

Chambers, Dewey W. *Literature for Children: The Oral Tradition; Storytelling and Creative Drama.* Dubuque, Iowa: William C. Brown Co., Publishers, 1977.

Colum, Padraic. *Storytelling New and Old.* New York: Macmillan Publishing Co., Inc., 1961.

Dorian, Margery, and Gulland, Frances. *Telling Stories through Movement.* Belmont, Calif.: Pittman Learning, 1974.

For Storytellers and Storytelling: Bibliography, Materials and Resource Aids. Chicago: American Library Association, 1968.

Gagliardo, Ruth. *Let's Read Aloud.* New York: J. B. Lippincott Co., 1962.

Glazer, Joan I., and Williams, Gurney, III. *Introduction to Children's Literature.* New York: McGraw-Hill Book Co., 1979.

Meeker, Alice M. *Enjoying Literature with Children.* New York: Odyssey Press, 1969.

Moore, Vardine. *Pre-School Story House.* Metuchen, N.J.: Scarecrow Press, Inc., 1972.

Ross, Ramon R. *Storyteller.* 2d. ed. Columbus, Ohio: Charles E. Merrill Publishing Co., 1980.

Sawyer, Ruth. *The Way of the Storyteller.* New York: Penguin Books, Inc., 1977.

Shedlock, Marie. *The Art of the Story-Teller.* New York: Dover Publications, Inc., 1951.

Children's Book References

Anonymous. *This Is the House that Jack Built.* In *Anthology of Children's Literature,* 5th ed., edited by Edna Johnson, Evelyn Shields, Frances Clarke Sayers, and Carolyn Horowitz. Boston: Houghton Mifflin Co., 1977.

Bodecker, N. M. *'Let's Marry!' Said the Cherry.* In *Anthology of Children's Literature,* 5th ed., edited by Edna Johnson, Evelyn Shields, Frances Clarke Sayers, and Carolyn Horowitz. Boston: Houghton Mifflin Co., 1977.

Briggs, Nancy, and Wagner, Joseph A. *Children's Literature through Storytelling and Drama.* Dubuque, Iowa: William C. Brown Co., Publishers, 1970.

Flack, Marjorie. *Ask Mr. Bear.* New York: Macmillan Publishing Co., Inc., 1971.

Gág, Wanda. *Millions of Cats.* New York: Coward-McCann, 1938.

Galdone, Paul. *The Gingerbread Boy.* New York: Seabury Press, Inc., 1975.

Keats, Ezra Jack. *Over in the Meadow.* New York: Scholastic Book Services, 1972.

Martin, Bill. *Brown Bear, Brown Bear, What Do You See?* Bill Martin's Instant Readers. New York: Holt, Rinehart and Winston, Inc., 1970.

Nelson, Mary Ann. *A Comparative Anthology of Children's Literature.* New York: Holt, Rinehart and Winston, Inc., 1972.

Seuss, Dr. *Horton Hatches the Egg.* New York: Random House, Inc., 1940.

Slobodkina, Esphyr. *Caps for Sale.* Glenview, Ill.: Addison-Wesley Publishing Co., Inc., 1947.

Will and Nicolas, pseud. *Finders Keepers.* New York: Harcourt Brace Jovanovich, Inc., 1951.

Zuromskis, Diane. *The Farmer in the Dell.* Boston: Little, Brown & Co., 1978.

4 READING ALOUD WITH YOUNG CHILDREN

Joan I. Glazer
Rhode Island College

The Importance of Reading Aloud

When planning a curriculum, both long-range and on a day-to-day basis, a teacher needs to be fully aware of the purposes for each activity or sequence of activities included. Often the only reason given for reading aloud to young children is that the children enjoy it. This is, of course, vital to a program of literature, but it overlooks the central role literature can play in children's development.

When children are introduced to the pleasure of literature, they often develop a desire to learn to read themselves. Chomsky (1972) found that the linguistic stage of development of prereaders was positively correlated to their having listened to books read aloud. Durkin (1966), in her study of children who read before entering school, found that *in every instance* the child had been read to by parents or older siblings. Children who have laughed at the antics of Curious George, gasped at some of Madeline's adventures, and empathized with Everett Anderson, know there are discoveries to be made on the pages of books. They are eager to be able to explore on their own, to be able to read.

Listening to literature read aloud enhances children's facility with language. They become familiar with the sound of literary language, styles of writing that may be more poetic or more metaphoric than the normal spoken word. In a picture book entitled *Beach Bird*, Carrick describes the beach as, "Sand drifted inland, pushed by the shoulder of the wind." When children hear words they know, such as "shoulder," being used in crea-tive ways, they are given the opportunity to expand their language horizons. As they hear characters in books speaking in dialects different from their own, they go beyond the language of their community to a broader understanding of language usages. They can begin to understand and appreciate the language used in the English folktale *Tom Tit Tot:* "Once upon a time there was a woman and she baked five pies. And when they came out of the oven, they were that overbaked the crusts were too hard to eat. So she says to her daughter, 'Darter,' says she, 'put you them there pies on the shelf, and leave 'em there a little, and they'll come again.' She meant, you know, the crust would get soft" (Ness, 1965). They know what Billy Jo Jive is talking about when he de-scribes two neighborhood basketball players: "Sneakers was a smoking bad dude. He was the star shooter for the 100th Street Jets. Steam Boat Louis was another bad dude. He was one of the heavies from the Bugaloo Smackers" (Shearer, 1977).

Several researchers (Blachowicz, 1978; Cazden, 1974; Holden and MacGinitie, 1972; Kavanagh and Mattingly, 1972) are exploring the development of children's metalinguistic awareness, that is, their ability to look at language forms con-sciously, seeing the form rather than the meaning. Children are doing this when they play language games, such as conversing in Pig Latin, or when they make up puns and riddles. They are also de-veloping metalinguistic awareness when they begin to recognize individual words within phrases or sentences, and individual sounds within words. Having children listen to stories appears to be one means of helping them become more aware of linguistic concepts, and of encouraging them to play with language themselves.

Facility with language is highly correlated with success in reading. Children are more likely to understand a printed word they have heard spoken than one they encounter for the first time in writing. The process of decoding becomes rewarding, with success marked by an understanding of what the print is "saying." Children who have listened to stories also are likely to have strong reading comprehension skills. Cohen (1968) reported that second graders in Harlem who heard and discussed literature regularly demonstrated increased vocabulary and reading comprehension over the control group that had not participated in the literature and reading activities. This coupling of desire to read with enhanced possibility of success in reading makes sharing literature aloud with children an indispensable prereading and beginning reading activity.

Not only the language of books, but the content as well can contribute to children's intellectual growth and breadth of knowledge. Through exposure to books children vicariously experience a variety of life-styles and family patterns. They encounter stories set in various regions of the United States and in foreign countries. There are books designed to present a specific concept, giving many concrete examples. Some books stimulate the imagination, taking children into the land of fantasy to explore unlimited possibilities. Others deal directly with emotions, telling of a child who is jealous of a new baby in the family, or sad and puzzled by the death of a grandparent. Each provides material for children's expanding knowledge of their world.

To explore a variety of family patterns, try sharing some of these stories with your students.

Caines, J. *Abby.* Illus. S. Kellogg. New York: Harper & Row, Publishers, Inc., 1973. (Adopted child)

Caines, J. *Daddy.* Illus. R. Himler. New York: Harper & Row, Publishers, Inc., 1977. (Child visiting divorced father)

Clifton, L. *Everett Anderson's 1-2-3.* Illus. A. Grifalconi. New York: Holt, Rinehart and Winston, Inc., 1977. (Mother planning remarriage)

Ehrlich, A. *Zeek Silver Moon.* Illus. R. Parker. New York: Dial Press, 1972. (Mother, father, one son)

Gray, G. *Send Wendell.* Illus. S. Shimin. New York: McGraw-Hill Book Co., 1974. (Mother, father, three children)

Lexau, J. *Benjie on His Own.* Illus. D. Bolognese. New York: Dial Press, 1972. (Grandmother, one child)

Lexau, J. *Emily and the Klunky Baby and the Next-Door Dog.* Illus. M. Alexander. New York: Dial Press, 1972. (Mother, two children)

Sonneborn, R. *Seven in a Bed.* Illus. D. Freeman. New York: Viking Press, 1968. (Mother, father, seven children)

Steptoe, J. *My Special Best Words.* New York: Viking Press, 1974. (Father, two children)

As children hear many fine stories and poems and as they observe the outstanding illustrations in high quality books, they begin to develop taste in literature and art. The sharing of well-written, well-illustrated books can be an introduction to aesthetic education.

Teachers have an opportunity to promote an awareness of literary and illustrative quality by asking children their reactions to certain books. They can plan reading aloud experiences so that the children hear a variety of literary genres, such as realistic fiction, fantasy, poetry, prose, nonfiction, and fiction.

To explore a variety of literary genre, try sharing some of these selections about dogs with your students.

Realism:

Carrick, C. *The Foundling.* New York: Houghton Mifflin Co., 1977.

Udry, J. *What Mary Jo Wanted.* Illus. E. Mill. Chicago: Albert Whitman & Co., 1968.

Fantasy:

Alexander, M. *Bobo's Dream.* New York: Dial Press, 1970.

Zion, G. *No Roses for Harry.* Illus. M. Graham. New York: Harper & Row, Publishers, Inc., 1958.

Poetry:

Asquith, M. "The Hairy Dog." In *Arrow Book of Poetry.* Edited by Ann McGovern. New York: Scholastic Book Services, 1965.

Chute, M. "Dogs." In *Poems Children Will Sit Still For.* Edited by de Regniers, Moore, and White. New York: Scholastic Book Services, 1969.

Nonfiction:

Selsam, M. *How Puppies Grow.* Illus. E. Bubley. New York: Scholastic Book Services, 1971.

Many books that preschool and primary-grade children enjoy hearing are too difficult for them to read independently. During the primary years, children's understanding far exceeds their ability to read. Literature is more likely to be enjoyed if it is presented by a skilled reader. Such a reader can emphasize meaning and the rhythm of the words, having passed the stage of struggling simply to pronounce the words. A smooth presentation shows children the power that literature can have.

Often after hearing a story, prereaders will "read" the book themselves, looking at the illustrations and recalling the story line. The reader has opened the world of literature to them. Somewhat older children, in the beginning stages of reading, will have their interest in literature kept alive as they listen to stories still beyond their reading capabilities. It is important to place books that have been read orally into the classroom library collection where children have easy and immediate access to them.

Reading to children is a shared experience that brings reader and listeners together emotionally and physically. There is a chance to talk about the content of the story, to point out what is seen in the illustrations, and to enjoy the security of being together. Reading aloud gives teacher and children something special to share such as a new set of friends that they all know, a joke they have all laughed at, or a time when nearly everyone cried. One second grade teacher began the school year by talking about *Where the Wild Things Are* with her new students. They had all heard it and all had opinions about it. Some called the wild things monsters and some referred to them as dinosaurs. Many remembered the first time they had seen the book. When the discussion ended, the teacher and children had begun to know each other and to feel that already they had something in common.

Reading aloud:

1. instills in children a desire to learn to read;

2. enhances their facility with language;

3. increases their chance of success in learning to read;

4. builds their vocabulary and comprehension skills;

5. increases their breadth of knowledge;

6. provides for aesthetic education;

7. allows the teacher to plan a balanced literature program;

8. helps keep interest in literature alive for children who are not yet reading at their understanding level;

9. encourages group cohesiveness.

The reasons for reading aloud, each important enough to justify the presentation of stories and poems, combine to show its importance even more strongly. A time for literature shared aloud belongs in the school as a regular and valued activity.

Criteria for Selecting Books

The first step in successful sharing of literature with children is the careful selection of books. Literary quality is of primary importance. With the myriad books available in public and school libraries, there is no reason not to choose the very best. You will want to look for books with well-constructed plots, ones in which the events are interrelated, and in which there is logical cause and effect. If the book is not a story as such, you will look for continuity, a rationale for what is shown and discussed. The writing style should be appropriate to the content of the book. Characters should be delineated so that the reader knows what the characters like and dislike, and how a given character might react in a new situation.

The illustrations, a major portion of the book, should be evaluated as carefully as the text. The medium used by the artist should be appropriate to the story. The artist should have captured the essence of the story, either portraying the text literally or expanding upon it for added dimension. In either case, the illustrations should not show anything that conflicts with the text.

Look at the format of the book, the way it is put together and the layout on each page. The pages should be visually pleasing. There should be enough space to make clear which picture illustrates which part of the text. The illustrations should appear either on the page or facing page with the text they portray.

Other considerations in selecting books are the audience and the reading situation. When reading to only one or two children at a time, you can use small books (5 × 8″ or less), such as *Don't Spill It Again, James* (Wells), where the illustrations can be easily seen. If the book is to be shared with a group, then a larger book should be chosen so listeners will be able to see the illustrations in enough detail to appreciate them. Jett-Simpson and Casey (1979) reported on a survey of second and fifth graders in which the students were asked to rate how they felt about certain teacher behaviors and activities related to literature. Of the 201 second graders, 80% liked having the teacher read every day; 82% liked having the teacher show the illustrations. For these children, seeing the illustrations was a vital part of the literary experience.

Whether reading to a few children or to a large group, the interests of the listeners should be kept in mind. Some topics, such as stories about animals, seem to be reliable favorites. Others may have appeal because they touch upon a special interest or mutual experience. You might share a book about the airport in preparation for a field trip there or upon the completion of such a trip. You might read a poem about a tornado, a blizzard, or a rain storm after such weather has been experienced.

Teachers must also choose books within the children's ability to understand. This does not mean that only the familiar can be presented. It does mean that there should be some point of contact, some common ground that will allow the children to make sense of what they hear. It may be that the setting is familiar; it may be that the situation is. Perhaps the children will relate to an emotion one of the characters is feeling. Five- and six-year-olds may have no idea where Peru is and may never have seen a llama when they hear *Ride the Cold Wind* (Surany). However, they will recognize Paco's feeling that what he is doing is dull, and that he really is old enough to go fishing on the lake, even though his father tells him he is too small. For very young children, the experience of being held while hearing the rhythm of beautiful sounding words may be enough.

The attention span of the children should be considered in determining how long a book to choose. In general, the older the child the longer the attention span is likely to be. However, attention is so related to interest that hard and fast rules cannot be made. Also, children may listen longer if they are given opportunities to participate in the reading by reciting a verse of a poem, or clapping, or if they are given a period for stretching and for talking between two short books or between chapters of a longer book.

Consider, as you are selecting books to be read aloud, that books contain powerful models of behavior for young children. One teacher read about *Pumpernickel Tickle and Mean Green Cheese* (Patz) to his first-grade class. This is a delightful story with imaginative wordplay about a boy and his elephant who go shopping and valiantly try to

remember the grocery list. In the middle of the book, Benji and Elephant get angry with each other for not remembering the list and call each other names. All is nicely resolved and the name calling consumes only a page of the book.

During recess later in the day you can guess what the first graders were doing. How might their name calling have been avoided? Perhaps the teacher could have discussed the name-calling episode and the way good feelings can accidentally turn bad. Perhaps he might have focused the children's attention on the wordplay, having them generate rhymes for their favorite foods. Or perhaps this would have been better presented as a lap story.

Many books for young children contain "in" behaviors, such as "putting one another down," showing off, or silliness. Other books may portray stereotypes. To avoid perpetuating these feelings and attitudes, scrutinize the books you select to read aloud.

The book chosen should be one that you like yourself. In that way you will be able to present it enthusiastically and honestly. And don't forget variety: the titles should include some that are humorous, some that are serious; some realism, some fantasy; some very new books, some classics. On occasion, when a book is popular with a child or a group of children, you will want to read it several times. Schickendanz (1978) suggests that the same story, if requested, should be read to an individual child several times, for through repetition the child masters the story line. This in turn allows the child to develop the general idea that story lines can be remembered, and to recognize in print those words and phrases that have been memorized. The child can construct an individual scheme for learning about reading. This requires that the teacher or an aide set aside time to read to individuals or to small groups, for not all children will be captivated by the same story.

You may want to read nursery rhymes and other poetry several times to the whole class, however, for these give more enjoyment when they are well known, just as music often becomes more appreciated through repetition.

As you select books, ask yourself the following questions:

1. Is the book of high literary and artistic quality?

2. Will the children understand the story?

3. Will the book interest the children?

4. Do I like the book myself?

5. If the book is to be shared with a group of children, are the illustrations large enough for them to see?

6. Does the book portray the behaviors and attitudes I condone for young children?

Techniques for Reading Aloud

Once the book or books have been selected, the next step is to practice reading them aloud, and to plan how you will present them. There are somewhat different techniques, depending on whether the book is to be shared with only one or two children, or with a larger group, perhaps the whole class. Books shared with only one or two are often termed "lap stories," and the sharing technique "lap reading."

Lap Reading

Many children experience lap reading at home as they sit on the lap of a parent or grandparent and listen to stories read aloud. However, not all do, and the importance of this early and intimate sharing of literature is such that teachers should provide for its inclusion in their program, particularly since so many children now come from homes where parents work and have less time for reading with them.

Reading aloud appears to be an effective method for helping children gain an overall gestalt of language, what it is and how it functions. It increases their capacity to distinguish separate phrases, words, and sounds in the context of full sentences. It provides an atmosphere for language growth as teachers and children talk together about the book.

Lap reading has been especially fruitful for learning disabled students who are mainstreamed and for young children who spend long hours in day-care facilities or public schools.

Not just that it *is* done, but *how* it is done, makes a difference. Flood (1977) studied the relationship between parental style of reading to young children and the children's performance on certain prereading related tasks. It can be assumed that styles found effective for parents would also be effective for teachers of young children. He found six items that were significantly related to the prereading score:

1. total number of words spoken by the child;

2. number of questions answered by the child;

3. number of questions asked by the child;

4. warm-up preparatory questions asked by the parents;

5. poststory evaluative questions asked by the parents;

6. positive reinforcement by the parents.

All show the importance of children's being actively involved with the story. Warm-up questions set the stage and help them anticipate what will happen. Children ask and answer questions during the story, and are encouraged in their responses. At the conclusion of the story, they have time to evaluate the experience, to integrate what was heard.

Some books lend themselves easily to this type of sharing, to an ongoing discussion as the book is read. Maczuga (1976) recommends books that include objects that can be discussed, alphabet books, and counting books. Also, books such as *Crash! Bang! Boom!* that invite the child to make sound effects are recommended. However, lap reading techniques can be applied to any book. Look for ways to introduce the story so that the child will talk about it before the reading begins. Try asking what the child expects the book to be about from looking at the cover, or soliciting a guess about what the title means. Look for ways to involve the child during the reading, such as repeating a refrain, describing an illustration, or predicting what will happen next.

Point as you read. For very young children, point to things in pictures as you talk about them. Pointing helps focus attention, thus lengthening the time children will sit still for a story. It also develops visual literacy, the idea that pictures have meaning.

Point to words, also. For younger children, such pointing will show them that those white spaces between words are word boundaries, an important concept. For beginning readers, pointing to words will allow them to read the words they know. You read most of the words, but stop and let the beginning reader supply those words he or she has learned. Gradually this "assisted reading" can progress to where you read a page and the child reads a page; this helps the transition to independent reading.

As with any other technique, pointing can be overdone. You can ruin a story by word calling instead of reading it. After the story has been read fluently once, though, it is often fun to go back over it and look at the words. Evidence suggests that teachers point too little rather than too much when lap reading, but don't overdo it. Also, children who are beginning to read enjoy skimming a story they have heard to find words they can read.

Very young children can help control the reading situation by turning the pages themselves, thus determining when they are ready to proceed with the story. Talk about unusual words, or about phrases the child does not understand. When the story is finished, ask questions that will lead the child to evaluate it, or compare it to personal experience. Don't limit your questions to whether the child liked the story or not. The response will be "yes" or "no" and all further thinking will be cut off.

Try these books in a lap reading session. See if you can actively involve the child in discussion.

For preschoolers:

Brown, M. *Goodnight Moon*. Illus. C. Hurd. New York: Harper & Row, Publishers, Inc., 1947.

Feder, J. *Beany*. New York: Pantheon Books, 1979.

Maestro, B. *Busy Day: A Book of Action Words*. New York: Crown Publishers, Inc., 1978.

Rockwell, H. *My Doctor*. New York: Macmillan Publishing Co., Inc., 1973.

For primary grade children:

Anno, M. *Anno's Journey*. New York: Philomel Books, 1978.

Raskin, E. *Nothing Ever Happens on My Block*. New York: Atheneum Publishers, 1966.

Scheer, J. *Rain Makes Applesauce*. Illus. M. Bileck. New York: Holiday House, Inc., 1964.

Spier, P. *Noah's Ark*. Garden City, N.Y.: Doubleday & Co., Inc., 1977.

Teacher judgment will be needed to assess the amount, type, and timing of questions. It is possible to ruin as well as to enhance a story through questioning and discussion. Yet having the child contribute thoughts and feelings about the story, or add to it through singing or saying parts of it with the reader, integrates the story more fully with the child's experience. It is a matter of recognizing both the potential of the literature and the interests of the listener.

Group Reading

Always read the book before sharing it orally with children. The idea that you must read a book a child has brought to school to avoid hurting that child's feelings is no excuse for unprepared oral reading. Explain to the child that you must practice to read aloud. Take the book home and read it. Then *share* only those parts suitable for the children in your class. You don't want to expose your class to poor literature. The story might be better read as a lap story to the child who brought it in.

It is useful not only to read the story, but also to practice reading the book orally before presenting it to children. You may find dialogue that you wish to dramatize, or special features of the language that you wish to highlight. You might tape-record yourself reading, then assess the quality of your voice, the expression and enunciation you have used, the speed and volume of your reading. When you are reading to children, be aware of their reactions, for these may give you insight into your oral reading strengths and weaknesses.

Several of the techniques of lap reading apply to group reading and vice versa. In group reading, as in lap reading, the introduction of the book sets the stage for the reading and should be such that children will want to hear the story.

A book may be introduced with the title and author, or with statements and questions about the book's content, or about how the book relates to something the children have experienced or discussed. Opening with the title often elicits the "I heard it before" comment, which can be handled with a statement recognizing the fact, but not dwelling on it. "Don't tell how it ends," or "See if you see something this time that you didn't see before" is sufficient. If the title is not given at the beginning, it should be given at the end. Author and illustrator should also be mentioned, for this gives children the realization that books are created by real people. You might also want to consider having group reading a choice activity rather than a required one.

If there are unfamiliar words that are essential to the understanding of the story, you may want to define them briefly, perhaps even parenthetically as they appear. Try asking the children directly what a word means if it is part of the title. If you were going to share *The Washout* with young children, it would be useful to discuss the meaning of "washout" with them before beginning the book. The cover illustration would help them discover the meaning of the word. If the book has so many unfamiliar words that there are going to be constant interruptions for explanation, then the book is probably too difficult for that listening audience. Many words that look difficult at the start are defined through context. There is no need to define "peddler" in *Caps for Sale* because the initial sentence reads, "Once there was a peddler who sold caps."

Try to maintain eye contact with the children, sharing the book in a more personal way, so that you can respond to their laughter or concern. In a practical sense, keeping an eye on your audience also allows you to predict trouble spots before trouble develops. A look from you may indicate that a toy is to be put away, with no interruption of the story, or a nod may excuse a child to go to the restroom.

Children should be seated so that all can see the reader and the book. This may be a semicircle, either on the floor or on chairs. If children are on the floor, you may want to be seated on a low chair so that the book is at eye level for the children; make sure children aren't craning their necks to look up. If the children are on chairs, you may choose to stand or to sit on a higher chair. Be sure to settle the children with a finger play or song, and be sure that they can see the illustrations before you begin. Some techniques teachers have used with little children to get them to sit still during story reading and not touch each other include having *each* child bring a rug sample to the circle to sit on or having children sit with crossed legs. The latter can get uncomfortable after awhile. Be sure to allow for stretches between stories, if you read more than one. Some teachers have mastered the art of reading upside down, so can hold the book in front of them and look down over the pages and read the text. Some hold the book off to one side, reading at an angle. A caution here is not to whip the book past the eyes of the children so fast that all that registers is a blur of color. It takes time to focus on an illustration, so the book should be moved slowly, if at all.

When the book is completed, children should be given a chance to respond if they wish. Sometimes children will spontaneously chime in after the story is over, but at other times the teacher will need to ask for a specific response. Open-ended questions generate more response than "yes" or "no" questions. Suggestions for activities that could extend the concepts of the book's language may be given. If the book is put in a special place that the children know, then they are encouraged to look at the book themselves later on. This gives the teacher an informal evaluation of which books are most liked, and of which children are showing an interest in literature.

Lamme has looked extensively at the skill of teachers and aides in reading aloud to young children. A conclusion of one study was that "reading aloud to a group of young children is an activity that requires training and/or experience to be done well." She found that there was a wide range of scores for both teachers and aides on the "Reading Aloud to Children Scale" (RACS, fig. 14) and that there was no relationship between the way a teacher read and the way the aide in that classroom read.

You may want to do some self-assessment by rating yourself on the RACS, reproduced in figure 14. You might videotape yourself reading to a group of young children, then code your own videotape. You might also find it a useful tool for self-training in oral reading. If there are items on which your rating was low (a or b of the multiple choice ratings, or repeated "no's" to the yes/no ratings), you should concentrate on improving in these areas. If you are working with an aide, student teacher, or volunteer, take time to help the aide develop skills in oral reading.

In another study, Lamme (1977) rated primary grade teachers' oral reading skills on a preliminary form of the RACS to determine which behaviors contributed most substantially to the quality of oral reading. In the order of influence, they were:

1. child involvement in the story reading;
2. amount of eye contact between reader and audience;
3. amount of expression put into the reading;
4. voice quality of the reader;
5. pointing to words of pictures by the reader;
6. reader's familiarity with the story;
7. selection of an appropriate book;
8. children being seated so that all can see;
9. highlighting of words and language by the reader.

These, as well as the rating scale, provided guidelines for the improvement of oral reading.

Reading Aloud to Children Scale (Revised)
(for use with picture story books)

Rater's Name: _____ School: _____

Date: _____ Grade Level: _____ Teacher: _____

Title of Story Being Read: _____

1. Does the adult introduce the book to the group?
   _____ a. None
   _____ b. Vague, "We're going to read this book."
   _____ c. More specific introduction, "Look at this book about a dog."
   _____ d. Specific introduction relating the book to the readers: "This book is about a lost dog like the dog in our schoolyard."

2. Title and Author
   Yes   No
   _____ _____ a. mentions title
   _____ _____ b. mentions author
   _____ _____ c. reads from cover
   _____ _____ d. reads from title page

3. Can all of the children in the group see the illustrations and hear the story?
   _____ a. Only a few children can see and/or hear.
   _____ b. At least half of the children can see and/or hear.
   _____ c. All but a few in the back or at the sides can see and hear.
   _____ d. *Every* child in the group can see and hear.

4. Reader's voice
   Yes   No
   _____ _____ a. Volume has variety (not too loud or soft).
   _____ _____ b. Speed has variety (not too fast or slow).
   _____ _____ c. Pitch has variety (not too high or low).
   _____ _____ d. Enunciation is clear.

5. Does the reader read with expression? Are emotions expressed?
   _____ a. The reading is monotonous.
   _____ b. There is some expression and feeling in parts of the story.
   _____ c. There is expression and emotion evidenced in much of the story.
   _____ d. There are vivid vocal and facial expressions; emotions appropriate to the story are in evidence (humor, empathy, etc.).

6. Are contents of the book suitable for the audience?
   _____ a. The book is either too sophisticated or too mundane; only a few children show interest in the book.
   _____ b. The book is of average appeal; children show some interest in it.
   _____ c. The book is appealing; most children like it.
   _____ d. The book is very appropriate for the age level and interests of the children; it has great appeal.

7. Are pictures visible to the children while the reader is reading?
   _____ a. The reader does not show the pictures to the group.
   _____ b. The reader stops to show pictures occasionally.
   _____ c. The reader pauses after each page to show pictures.
   _____ d. The reader holds the book so that the children can look at pictures *while* the story is being read.

8. How familiar is the reader with the story?
   _____ a. Not at all. The reader must read the story word for word.

_____ b. There is some familiarity with the story but most of the words need to be read; some words are read on every page.

_____ c. The reader knows the story but must occasionally refer to the text; at least one page is told rather than read.

_____ d. The reader is thoroughly familiar with the story and reads with little or no reference to the book.

9. Is the reader highlighting words and the quality of language unique to this selection (noticing rhyming words, unusual words ["curious" George], refrains, repetition of phrases or words; changing voice of expression for those language elements)?

_____ a. There is little notice given to language or vocabulary in the reading.

_____ b. There is some notice given to language or vocabulary.

_____ c. The language element is evident in the story reading.

_____ d. The language element is *very* evident in the story reading.

10. Further activities

Yes   No

_____ _____ a. suggests further student involvement with book or topic

_____ _____ b. leaves the book where children could return to it

_____ _____ c. asks an interpretive question about the story (not recall of facts)

_____ _____ d. returns to the book for a review of the story (shows pictures again, recalls an event, etc.)

Coding

Put a mark each time the behavior occurs.

_____ Times reader points to things in picture

_____ Times reader points to words

_____ Times reader demonstrates left-right progression

_____ Times teacher initiates student response to story

_____ Times students initiate response to story

_____ Times reader looks up from book at audience

Figure 14. Reading aloud to children scale (revised).

Whether lap reading or group reading, the teacher should work to become a skilled oral reader, and to involve children actively with the literature. The adult should also be aware of and should respect children's responses and moods. If a story is disliked, it can be abandoned and another one chosen. Sometimes children need to talk about their feelings after a book; other times they need a quiet period for their own thoughts.

As you read aloud to and with children, you are helping those children establish lifetime habits of reading and positive attitudes toward literature. It is time well spent.

Professional References

Blachowicz, C. "Metalinguistic Awareness and the Beginning Reader." *The Reading Teacher* 31 (1978): 875-876.

Cazden, C. "Play and Metalinguistic Awareness: One Dimension of Language Experience." *Urban Review* 7 (1974): 28-39.

Chomsky, C. "Stages in Language Development and Reading Exposure." *Harvard Educational Review* 42 (1972): 1-33.

Cohen, D. "The Effect of Literature on Vocabulary and Reading Achievement." *Elementary English* 45 (1968): 209-213.

Durkin, D. *Children Who Read Early.* New York: Teachers College Press, 1966.

Flood, J. "Parental Styles in Reading Episodes with Young Children." *The Reading Teacher* 30 (1977): 864-867.

Holden, M. H., and MacGinitie, W. H. "Children's Conceptions of Word Boundaries in Speech and Print." *Journal of Educational Psychology* 63 (1972): 551-557.

Jett-Simpson, M., and Casey, J. Paper presented at the National Council of Teachers of English Conference on the Language Arts in the Elementary School, March 24, 1979, Hartford, Connecticut.

Kavanagh, J. F., and Mattingly, I. G., eds. *Language by Ear and by Eye: The Relationships between Speech and Reading.* Cambridge, Mass.: MIT Press, 1972.

Lamme, L. "Reading Aloud to Children." *Language Arts* 53 (1976): 886-888.

Lamme, L. "Reading Aloud to Children: A Comparative Study of Teachers and Aides." Unpublished research report, 1977.

Maczuga, A. "Lap Books for Family Sharing." *Top of the News,* Fall (1976): 89-91.

Schickedanz, J. " 'Please Read That Story Again!' Exploring Relationships between Story Reading and Learning to Read." *Young Children* 33 (1978): 48-55.

Children's Book References

Carrick, C. *Beach Bird.* New York: Dial Press, 1973.

Carrick, C. *The Washout.* New York: Houghton Mifflin Co., 1978.

Ness, E. *Tom Tit Tot.* New York: Charles Scribner's Sons, 1965.

Patz, N. *Pumpernickle Tickle and Mean Green Cheese.* New York: Franklin Watts, Inc., 1978.

Sendak, M. *Where the Wild Things Are.* New York: Harper & Row, Publishers, Inc., 1963.

Shearer, J. *Billy Jo Jive: Super Private Eye. The Case of the Sneaker Snatcher.* Illus. T. Shearer. New York: Dell Publishing Co., Inc., 1977.

Slobodkina, E. *Caps for Sale.* New York: Addison-Wesley Publishing Co., Inc., 1947.

Spier, P. *Crash! Bang! Boom!* New York: Doubleday & Co., Inc., 1972.

Surany, A. *Ride the Cold Wind.* New York: G. P. Putnam's Sons, 1964.

Wells, R. *Don't Spill It Again, James.* New York: Dial Press, 1977.

Related Readings

Bamman, Henry A.; Dawson, Mildred; and Whitehead, Robert J. *Oral Interpretation of Children's Literature.* 2d ed. Dubuque, Iowa: William C. Brown Co., Publishers, 1971.

Chan, Julie. *Why Read Aloud to Children?* Newark, Del.: International Reading Association, 1974.

Cianciolo, Patricia, ed. *Picture Books for Children.* Chicago: American Library Association, 1973.

Coody, Betty. *Using Literature with Young Children.* Dubuque, Iowa: William C. Brown Co., Publishers, 2d ed., 1979.

Duff, Annis. *"Bequest of Wings": A Family's Pleasure with Books.* New York: Viking Press, 1944.

Glazer, Joan, and Williams, Gurney, III. *Introduction to Children's Literature.* New York: McGraw-Hill Book Co., 1979.

Huck, Charlotte S. *Children's Literature in the Elementary School,* 3rd ed. New York: Holt, Rinehart and Winston, Inc., 1976.

Jacobs, Leland B., ed. *Using Literature with Young Children.* New York: Teachers College Press, 1965.

Johnson, Ferne, ed. *Start Early for an Early Start: You and the Young Child.* Chicago: American Library Association, 1976.

Lanes, Selma G. *Down the Rabbit Hole: Adventures and Misadventures in the Realm of Children's Literature.* New York: Atheneum Publishers, 1971.

Larrick, Nancy. *A Parent's Guide to Children's Reading.* 4th ed. New York: Doubleday & Co., Inc., 1975.

Moore, Vardine. *Pre-School Story Hour.* 2d ed. Metuchen, N.J.: Scarecrow Press, Inc., 1972.

Painter, Helen W. *Poetry and Children.* Newark, Delaware: International Reading Association, 1970.

Sims, Rudine. "Reading Literature Aloud." In *Literature and Young Children.* Edited by Bernice Cullinan and Carolyn Carmichael. Urbana, Ill.: National Council of Teachers of English, 1977.

Sutherland, Zena, and Arbuthnot, May Hill. *Children and Books.* 6th ed. Glenview, Ill.: Scott, Foresman & Co., 1981.

5 LITERATURE THROUGHOUT THE CURRICULUM

Linda Leonard Lamme
University of Florida

The previous chapters developed numerous ideas for using literature for its own sake—through activities such as storytelling, drama, puppetry, and S.S.R. While these activities, in and of themselves, are worthwhile, literature can contribute a great deal more to an early childhood program. This chapter will present ways to integrate literature into the entire curriculum, putting the previously-mentioned strategies to use in a meaningful framework.

If a literature routine is already established in your classroom, integrating literature into other curricular areas won't be difficult. Basically it requires a mind-set that says, "What book, story, poem, or song would add to our enjoyment of and learning about this topic?" One excellent source, Jacob's *Independent Reading Grades One through Three: An Annotated Bibliography with Reading Levels,* lists books for young children by topic and reading level. Many public libraries create topical lists for their patrons. EDMARC (The Education Materials Center, 400 Maryland Ave. S.W., Washington, D.C. 20202) will provide lists of recent books on virtually any topic for a minimal charge.

Books can be the springboard into or the culmination of a unit of study, or aids during the study of a topic. Examples may be found in the following chapter where individual teachers describe ways they have used literature in their classrooms.

You will want to include literature in all curricular areas for affective as well as cognitive reasons. *The Bookfinder* (1977) is an excellent source of review of books on many affective themes (divorce, adoption, friendship, emotions, etc.).

Literature in Curricular Areas

An early childhood program typically includes the following curricular areas: mathematics, language arts, reading, science, social studies, art, music, and physical education. Teachers also provide for manipulative activities, such as cooking, sand and water play, and dressups. Literature can fit into each of these topics. Then, there are special occasions and circumstances that literature can help celebrate. Ways to involve children with literature in each of these areas follow.

Mathematics

There are many picture books published at the early childhood level that have as their goal teaching young children mathematical concepts. Counting books are the most common. An appropriate counting book for young children has clearly identified items to be counted, pictures in proper perspectives (not bees larger than airplanes), numerals both written in words and in number form, and different opportunities to count the same number of items on a page. *Anno's Counting Book,* for example, begins with zero (often omitted in counting books) and has on each page many groups exemplifying the appropriate numeral (three clouds, three trees, etc.).

The following counting books meet these criteria.

Anno, Mitsumasa. *Anno's Counting Book.* New York: Thomas Y. Crowell Co., 1977.

Bayley, Nicola. *One Old Oxford.* New York: Atheneum Publishers, 1977.

Brown, Marc. *One Two Three: An Animal Counting Book.* Boston: Atlantic Monthly Press, 1976.

Carle, Eric. *1,2,3 to the Zoo*. New York: Philomel Books, 1968.

Francoise, C. *Jeanne-Marie Counts Her Sheep*. New York: Charles Scribner's Sons, 1957.

Freschet, Berniece. *The Ants Go Marching*. Illus. Stefan Martin. New York: Charles Scribner's Sons, 1973.

Fujikawa, Gyo. *Can You Count?* New York: Grosset & Dunlap, Inc., 1977.

Hoban, Tana. *Count and See*. New York: Macmillan Publishing Co., Inc., 1972.

Howard, Katherine. *I Can Count to 100—Can You?* Illus. Michael J. Smollin. New York: Random House, Inc., 1979.

Yolen, Jane. *An Invitation to the Butterfly Ball: A Counting Rhyme*. Illus. Jane Breskin Zalben. New York: Parents Magazine Press, 1976.

Other mathematical concepts are the focus of books.

Eastman, P. D. *What Time Is It?* New York: Random House, Inc., 1979.

Hoban, Tana. *Push, Pull, Empty, Full: A Book of Opposites*. New York: Macmillan Publishing Co., Inc., 1972.

Hoban, Tana. *Circles, Triangles and Squares*. New York: Macmillan Publishing Co., Inc., 1974.

Hutchins, Pat. *Clocks and More Clocks*. New York: Macmillan Publishing Co., Inc., 1970.

Reiss, John J. *Shapes*. New York: Bradbury Press, 1974.

Spier, Peter. *Fast-Slow, High-Low: A Book of Opposites*. New York: Doubleday & Co., Inc., 1972.

Mathematical concepts are also covered incidentally in picture books for young children. For example, youngsters can learn to measure with the inchworm in *Inch by Inch*. Incidental mathematical learning probably occurs frequently when books are shared with young children.

Language Arts

There are three areas of language acquisition that can be enhanced by literature: phonology (the sounds of language), syntax (the structure of language), and semantics (the meaning of language). All books model language to some degree, but some more obviously emphasize one of these areas.

Rhyming literature—poetry, songs, and stories with refrains—all enhance phonology. Books that involve word play, like *Pumpernickel Tickle and Mean Green Cheese*, help children learn to rhyme and invent words. Here are a number of books that focus, either directly or indirectly, on phonology (the sounds of language).

Bayley, Nicola. *Nicola Bayley's Book of Nursery Rhymes*. New York: Alfred A. Knopf, Inc., 1977.

de Regniers, Beatrice S. *May I Bring a Friend?* Illus. Beni Montresor. New York: Atheneum Publishers, 1964.

Frost, Robert. *Stopping by Woods on a Snowy Evening*. Illus. Susan Jeffers. New York: E. P. Dutton, 1978.

Fujikawa, Gyo. *Mother Goose*. New York: Grosset & Dunlap, Inc., 1968.

Hopkins, Lee Bennett. *Go to Bed! A Book of Bedtime Poems*. Illus. Rosekrans Hoffman. New York: Alfred A. Knopf, Inc., 1979.

Kuskin, Karla. *A Boy Had a Mother Who Brought Him a Hat*. Boston: Houghton Mifflin Co., 1976.

Langstaff, John. *Hot Cross Buns and Other Old Street Cries*. Illus. Nancy Winslow Parker. New York: Atheneum Publishers, 1978.

Lear, Edward. *The Owl and the Pussy Cat and Other Nonsense*. Illus. Owen Wood. New York: Viking Press, 1979.

McCord, David. *Every Time I Climb a Tree*. Illus. Marc Simont. Boston: Little, Brown & Co., 1967.

Rojankovsky, Feodor. *Tall Book of Mother Goose*. New York: Harper & Row, Publishers, Inc., 1942.

Stevenson, Robert Louis. *A Child's Garden of Verses*. Illus. Brian Wildsmith. New York: Franklin Watts, Inc., 1966.

Tudor, Tasha. *Mother Goose*. New York: Henry Z. Walck, Inc., 1944.

Wildsmith, Brian. *Brian Wildsmith's Mother Goose*. New York: Franklin Watts, Inc., 1965.

Wright, Blanche. *The Real Mother Goose*. Chicago, Ill.: Rand McNally & Co., 1978.

Syntax is strengthened by books that repeat language patterns the children are acquiring. Look for books that repeat prepositional phrases, dependent clauses, adjectives and adverbs, questions, and sentences.

Arno, Ed. *The Gingerbread Man*. New York: Scholastic Book Services, 1970.

Baum, Arline, and Baum, Joseph. *One Bright Monday Morning*. New York: Random House, Inc., 1962.

Blair, Susan. *The Three Billy Goats Gruff*. New York: Scholastic Book Services, 1970.

Emberley, Barbara. *Drummer Hoff*. Illus. Ed Emberley. Englewood Cliffs, N.J.: Prentice-Hall, Inc., 1967.

Galdone, Paul. *The Three Billy Goats Gruff*. New York: Seabury Press, Inc., 1973.

Galdone, Paul. *The Gingerbread Boy*. New York: Seabury Press, Inc., 1975.

Galdone, Paul. *Three Little Pigs*. New York: Seabury Press, Inc., 1970.

Galdone, Paul. *The Three Bears*. New York: Seabury Press, Inc., 1972.

Galdone, Paul. *The Little Red Hen.* New York: Seabury Press, Inc., 1973.

Heilbroner, Joan. *This Is the House Where Jack Lives.* Illus. Aliki. New York: Harper & Row, Publishers, Inc., 1962.

Hutchins, Pat. *Good-Night Owl.* New York: Macmillan Publishing Co., Inc., 1972.

Hutchins, Pat. *Rosie's Walk.* New York: Macmillan Publishing Co., Inc., 1968.

McGovern, Ann. *Stone Soup.* Illus. Nola Langner. New York: Scholastic Book Services, 1971.

McGovern, Ann. *Too Much Noise.* Illus. Simms Taback. Boston: Houghton Mifflin Co., 1967.

Sendak, Maurice. *Chicken Soup with Rice.* New York: Harper & Row, Publishers, Inc., 1962.

Shaw, Charles G. *It Looked Like Spilt Milk.* New York: Harper & Row, Publishers, Inc., 1947.

Soule, Jean C. *Never Tease a Weasel.* New York: Parents Magazine Press, 1964.

Tanz, Christine. *An Egg Is to Sit On.* Illus. Rosekrans Hoffman. New York: Lothrop, Lee & Shepard Books, 1978.

Books that enhance semantic language development help children's vocabulary grow or aid in giving meaning to language in other ways. Plays on the meanings of words, homonyms, synonyms, and antonyms would be included in this category.

Farber, Norma. *As I Was Crossing Boston Common.* Illus. Arnold Lobel. New York: E. P. Dutton, 1975.

Hoberman, Mary Ann. *A House Is a House for Me.* Illus. Betty Fraser. New York: Viking Press, 1978.

Parish, Peggy. *Teach Us, Amelia Bedelia.* Illus. Lynn Sweat. New York: Greenwillow Books, 1977.

Provensen, Alice, and Provensen, Martin. *A Peaceable Kingdom: The Shaker Abecedarius.* New York: Viking Press, 1978.

Reading

The study of good literature provides young children with abundant opportunities to develop reading readiness and reading skills. Book awareness skills, including left–right progression, can be learned using the following books:

Carle, Eric. *Do You Want to Be My Friend?* New York: Thomas Y. Crowell Co., 1971.

Provensen, Alice, and Provensen, Martin. *A Peaceable Kingdom: The Shaker Abecedarius.* New York: Viking Press, 1978.

Wordless picture books that tell a story visually also encourage sequential page-turning. Visual discrimination is likewise encouraged by wordless books as well as books that play games with the pictures.

Ahlberg, Janet, and Ahlberg, Allen. *Each Peach, Pear, Plum: An I-Spy Story.* New York: Viking Press, 1978.

Anno, Mitsumasa. *Anno's Journey.* New York: Philomel Books, 1978.

Brown, Margaret Wise. *The Runaway Bunny.* Illus. Clement Hurd. New York: Harper & Row, Publishers, Inc., 1972.

Hoban, Tana. *Look Again.* New York: Macmillan Publishing Co., Inc., 1971.

Kellogg, Steven. *The Mystery of the Missing Red Mitten.* New York: Dial Press, 1974.

Books with sound effects expose young children to *auditory discrimination.* Also, any of the books that encourage oral language can be listed here.

Brown, Margaret Wise. *Country Noisy Book.* Illus. Leonard Weisgard. New York: Harper & Row, Publishers, Inc., 1940. Paperback edition, 1976.

Brown, Margaret Wise. *Noisy Book.* Illus. Leonard Weisgard. New York: Harper & Row, Publishers, Inc., 1939.

Spier, Peter. *Gobble, Growl, Grunt.* Garden City, N.Y.: Doubleday & Co., Inc., 1971.

Any book, of course, helps a child learn to read naturally if adults and/or older children share books and read to each other regularly. Lap reading by a skilled reader who points to words and discusses content and who is very responsive to the young child is probably the most effective method for teaching reading.

Science

Science books for young children are basically of two types. There are nonfiction factual accounts written at relatively easy reading levels or there are fiction books with scientific accuracy. When selecting science books to use with a science topic it is important to be sure the scientific information contained in the book is accurate. The book's illustrations should either be photographs or clear, realistic drawings.

Science, in early childhood education, is often referred to as "inquiry and discovery." It focuses on the processes of questioning, reasoning, discovering, and using the scientific method, rather than on memorizing facts about the physical environment. Science trade books, on the other hand, tend to preach and to teach facts. Although factual books are interesting and provide useful information, their use in an early childhood curriculum might best be in response to specific questions children ask rather than for group or independent reading.

The key question to ask when selecting a book to use and considering techniques for involving children with that book is, "Does the book contribute to a 'sense of wonder' about the world in which we live?" The following books are representative of books that young children enjoy and that offer multiple opportunities for integration into a science curriculum.

Aliki. *My Five Senses.* New York: Thomas Y. Crowell Co., 1972.

Ames, Gerald, and Wyler, Rose. *Prove It!* New York: Harper & Row, Publishers, Inc., 1963.

Asimov, Isaac. *Animals of the Bible.* Illus. Howard Berelson. Garden City, N.Y.: Doubleday & Co., Inc., 1978.

Barton, Byron. *Wheels.* New York: Thomas Y. Crowell Co., 1979.

Baylor, Byrd. *Everybody Needs a Rock.* Illus. Peter Parnall. New York: Charles Scribner's Sons, 1974.

Ets, Marie Hall. *Gilberto and the Wind.* New York: Viking Press, 1963.

Fisher, Aileen. *Going Barefoot.* Illus. Adrienne Adams. New York: Thomas Y. Crowell Co., 1960.

Fisher, Aileen. *Once We Went on a Picnic.* Illus. Tony Chen. New York: Thomas Y. Crowell Co., 1975.

Fisher, Aileen. *We Went Looking.* Illus. Marie Angel. New York: Thomas Y. Crowell Co., 1968.

Garelick, May. *Where Does the Butterfly Go When It Rains?* Illus. Leonard Weisgard. Reading, Mass.: Addison-Wesley Publishing Co., Inc., 1961.

Ginsburg, Mirra. *Mushroom in the Rain.* New York: Macmillan Publishing Co., Inc., 1978.

Goffstein, M. B. *Natural History.* New York: Farrar, Straus & Giroux, Inc., 1979.

Goldin, Augusta. *Spider Silk.* Illus. Joseph Low. New York: Thomas Y. Crowell Co., 1964.

Norris, Louanne, and Smith, Howard E., Jr. *An Oak Tree Dies and a Journey Begins.* Illus. Allen Davis. New York: Crown Publishers, Inc., 1979.

Perkins, Al. *Ear Book.* Illus. William O'Brian. New York: Random House, Inc., 1968.

Social Studies

Social studies concepts in early childhood focus on processes rather than facts. Young children's moral development has been studied by Damon (1977), who has delineated stages of moral development through which all children pass, though at very different rates depending upon the opportunities the child has been given for decision-making. The early childhood curriculum needs to expose children to moral dilemmas that are solved at a level just above where the child is. Children's literature abounds with opportunities for enhancing moral development in such areas as sharing, taking turns, preparing for a new baby, friendship and cooperation, sibling rivalry, and many others. Each of the following books contains a moral dilemma and is suitable for this type of social studies involvement.

Cohen, Miriam. *Will I Have a Friend?* Illus. Lillian Hoban. New York: Macmillan Publishing Co., Inc., 1967. Paperback edition, 1971.

Delaney, Ned. *Bert and Barney.* Boston: Houghton Mifflin Co., 1979.

Hamilton, Morse, and Hamilton, Emily. *My Name Is Emily.* Illus. Jenni Oliver. New York: Greenwillow Books, 1979.

Keats, Ezra Jack. *Peter's Chair.* New York: Harper & Row, Publishers, Inc., 1967.

Mahy, Margaret. *The Boy Who Was Followed Home.* Illus. Steven Kellogg. New York: Franklin Watts, Inc., 1975.

Roche, P. K. *Good-Bye, Arnold.* New York: Dial Press, 1979.

Turkle, Brinton. *Rachel and Obadiah.* New York: E. P. Dutton, 1978.

Waber, Bernard. *Ira Sleeps Over.* Boston: Houghton Mifflin Co., 1972.

Zolotow, Charlotte. *If It Weren't for You.* Illus. Ben Shecter. New York: Harper & Row, Publishers, Inc., 1966.

The more traditional topics of community helpers, history, geography, economics, etc. are not ignored by the process curriculum. Children learn about historic times, employment opportunities, and the like by dramatization, field trips, and active participation. They get the "feel" of other times, places, and cultures and do not simply memorize facts. Each of the following books goes well beyond the mere recitation of facts to provide young children with ideas they can actually use through role play and active involvement.

Baker, Betty. *Little Runner of the Longhouse.* New York: Harper & Row, Publishers, Inc., 1962.

Burton, Virginia. *Mike Mulligan and His Steam Shovel.* Boston: Houghton Mifflin Co., 1939. Paperback edition, 1977.

Hall, Donald. *Ox-Cart Man.* Illus. Barbara Cooney. New York: Viking Press, 1979.

Lindgren, Astrid. *Christmas in the Stable.* Illus. H. Wiberg. New York: Coward, McCann & Geoghegan, Inc., 1962.

Lowrey, Janette Sebring. *Six Silver Spoons.* Illus. Robert Quackenbush. New York: Harper & Row, Publishers, Inc., 1971.

McCloskey, Robert. *One Morning in Maine.* New York: Viking Press, 1952.

McCloskey, Robert. *Make Way for Ducklings.* New York: Viking Press, 1941.

Monjo, F. N. *The Drinking Gourd.* New York: Harper & Row, Publishers, Inc., 1969.

Table 1

Illustrative Media and Some Representative Illustrators*

Medium	Representative Illustrators
Photography	Tana Hoban Patricia Ruban Roger Bester Thomas Mattieson
Woodcut or Linocut	Don Freeman Marie Hall Ets Ed Emberley Evaline Ness Marcia Brown
Collage	Leo Lionni Ezra Jack Keats Eric Carle
Paint**	Tomi de Paola Ludwig Bemelmans Leo Politi Tasha Tudor Maurice Sendak Robert McCloskey Tony Chen William Pène du Bois Leonard Weisgard Roger Duvoisin Brian Wildsmith Alice and Martin Provensen Celestino Piatti Bruno Munari Nonny Hogrogian
Line Drawing	Glen Rounds
Crayon	Feodor Rojankovsky
Colored Pencil	Susan Jeffers Taro Yashima

* No quality judgments are being made here. Many excellent illustrators use a variety of media and therefore are not included in our list.

** Paint includes watercolor, tempera, postercolor, pastels, gouache, oil, and other paints. Paint is the most common way children's books are illustrated. Many painters combine paint with other media, such as pen and ink.

Art

Young children enjoy actively participating in art experiences while at the same time learning about art concepts of color (value), texture, line, movement, and direction. Children's books are the only artwork young children see, so it is important for teachers to use books of artistic quality. Caldecott Medal books and Children's Showcase Books have received awards for their high quality artwork.

Children need involvement with books illustrated in a variety of media. Cianciolo's *Illustrations in Children's Books* (1970) describes the many processes that are used to illustrate children's books, so if you can't identify the medium, you might want to consult that source. Table 1 will help you find books by illustrators who have received recognition for their work.

Creative teachers have developed many types of art projects using children's literature as a springboard. One second-grade teacher had her class make a quilt for the wall of the school media center. Each child made a colorful square from his or her favorite book. Teachers often have children make books patterned after real ones. Children can make dioramas, peep shows, puppets, and all of the materials mentioned in chapter three. These would qualify as art projects only if children could experience the processes of creation rather than imitation.

Music

Creating sound is a natural part of early childhood. Singing, dancing, moving, and soundmaking are all included in an early childhood curriculum, and each is enhanced by children's literature. Lamme (1979) has critiqued over sixty song picture books and provided ideas for using them with children of all ages. Young children might particularly enjoy:

Lullabies

Aliki. *Hush Little Baby.* Englewood Cliffs, N.J.: Prentice-Hall, Inc., 1968.

Zemach, Margot. *Hush Little Baby.* New York: E. P. Dutton, 1975.

Holiday Songs

Child, L. M. *Over the River and through the Wood.* Illus. Brinton Turkle. New York: Coward, McCann & Geoghegan, Inc., 1974.

Keats, Ezra Jack. *The Little Drummer Boy.* New York: Macmillan Publishing Co., Inc., 1968.

Kent, Jack. *Jack Kent's Twelve Days of Christmas.* New York: Parents Magazine Press, 1973.

Nursery Rhymes

Spier, Peter. *London Bridge Is Falling Down.* Garden City, N.Y.: Doubleday & Co., Inc., 1967.

Quackenbush, Robert. *Old MacDonald Had a Farm.* New York: J. B. Lippincott Co., 1972.

Quackenbush, Robert. *Pop! Goes the Weasel and Yankee Doodle: New York in 1776 and Today, with Songs and Pictures.* New York: J. B. Lippincott Co., 1976.

Zuromskis, Diane. *The Farmer in the Dell.* Boston: Little, Brown & Co., 1978.

Counting Rhymes

Adams, Adrianne. *This Old Man.* New York: Grosset & Dunlap, Inc., 1975.

Conover, Chris. *Six Little Ducks.* New York: Thomas Y. Crowell Co., 1976.

Keats, Ezra Jack. *Over in the Meadow.* New York: Scholastic Book Services, 1972.

Langstaff, John. *Over in the Meadow.* Illus. Feodor Rojankovsky. New York: Harcourt Brace Jovanovich, Inc., 1957. Paperback edition, 1973.

Silly Songs

Kellogg, Steven. *There Was an Old Woman.* New York: Scholastic Book Services, Inc., 1980.

Langstaff, John. *Oh, A-Hunting We Will Go.* Illus. Nancy Winslow Parker. New York: Atheneum Publishers, 1974.

Spier, Peter. *Fox Went Out on a Chilly Night.* Garden City, N.Y.: Doubleday & Co., Inc., 1961.

Folk Songs

Langstaff, John. *Ol' Dan Tucker.* Illus. J. Krush. New York: Harcourt Brace Jovanovich, Inc., 1963.

Parker, R. A. *Sweet Betsy from Pike: A Song from the Goldrush Days.* New York: Viking Press, 1978.

Quackenbush, Robert. *Skip to My Lou.* New York: J. B. Lippincott Co., 1975.

Quackenbush, Robert. *She'll Be Comin' 'round the Mountain.* New York: J. B. Lippincott Co., 1973.

Historical Songs

Bangs, Edward. *Yankee Doodle.* Illus. Steven Kellogg. New York: Scholastic Book Services, 1980.

Spier, Peter. *The Erie Canal.* Garden City, N.Y.: Doubleday & Co., Inc., 1970.

Alphabet Songs

Provensen, Alice, and Provensen, Martin. *A Peaceable Kingdom: The Shaker Abecedarius.* New York: Viking Press, 1978.

Yolen, Jane. *All in the Woodland Early: An ABC Book.* Illus. Jane Breskin Zalben. Cleveland: William Collins Publishers, Inc., 1979.

Many of these books have accompanying recordings or cassettes, published by Weston Woods, Weston, Connecticut. Song books with collections of songs could also be used. The emphasis in an early childhood curriculum would not be on

memorizing the songs or learning a formal dance or movement game, but rather on creating sounds—by singing and making up new tunes or lyrics, by moving to the music in varying ways (not imitating an adult), by beating rhythms and creating pitches with sound starters and quality musical instruments.

Several books involve instruments and sound effects.

Carle, Eric. *I See a Song.* New York: Thomas Y. Crowell Co., 1973.

Isadora, Rachel. *Ben's Trumpet.* New York: Greenwillow Books, 1979.

Spier, Peter. *Crash! Bang! Boom!* Garden City, N.Y.: Doubleday & Co., Inc., 1972.

Physical Education

Movement activities form the core of an early childhood physical education program. Young children learn gradually to gain more control over their bodies and individual parts of their bodies. Literature is an integral part of the physical education program through the use of finger plays, chants, and movement songs. Seldom do these appear as books for young children, but collections for teachers might include the following.

Glazer, Tom. *Eye Winker, Tom Tinker, Chin Chopper: A Collection of Musical Finger Plays.* Garden City, N.Y.: Doubleday & Co., Inc., 1973.

Glazer, Tom. *Do Your Ears Hang Low?* Garden City, N.Y.: Doubleday & Co., Inc., 1980.

Books sometimes reflect topics requiring physical movements or sports.

Bulla, Clyde Robert. *Keep Running Allen!* Illus. Satomi Ichikawa. New York: Thomas Y. Crowell Co., 1978.

Kessler, Leonard. *On Your Mark, Get Set, Go!* New York: Harper & Row, Publishers, Inc., 1972.

Krementz, Jill. *A Very Young Gymnast.* New York: Alfred A. Knopf, Inc., 1978.

McCord, David. *Every Time I Climb a Tree.* Illus. Marc Simont. Boston: Little, Brown & Co., 1967.

Phleger, F., and Phleger, M. *Off to the Races.* New York: Random House, Inc., 1968.

Cooking

Cooking has traditionally been a part of an early childhood curriculum for many reasons. When cooking, young children typically use all of their five physical senses. Cooking is a high involvement activity. Many teachers relate cooking to reading by making chart recipes or individual cookbooks for young children to share with their parents.

There are many children's cookbooks on the market. In addition, cooking activities can be a natural result of reading certain children's books.

Asche, Frank. *Good Lemonade.* New York: Franklin Watts, Inc., 1976.

Asche, Frank. *Sand Cake.* New York: Parents Magazine Press, 1979.

Brandenberg, Franz. *Fresh Cider and Pie.* New York: Macmillan Publishing Co., Inc., 1973.

Brown, Marcia. *Stone Soup.* New York: Charles Scribner's Sons, 1947.

Carle, Eric. *Pancakes, Pancakes.* New York: Alfred A. Knopf, Inc., 1970.

Carle, Eric. *The Very Hungry Caterpillar.* New York: Philomel Books, 1969.

Dalgliesh, Alice. *The Thanksgiving Story.* New York: Charles Scribner's Sons, 1954.

de Paola, Tomie. *Pancakes for Breakfast.* New York: Harcourt Brace Jovanovich, Inc., 1978.

de Regniers, Beatrice S. *May I Bring a Friend?* Illus. Beni Montresor. New York: Atheneum Publishers, 1964.

Galdone, Paul. *The Gingerbread Boy.* New York: Houghton Mifflin Co., 1975.

Galdone, Paul. *The Little Red Hen.* New York: Houghton Mifflin Co., 1973.

Hoban, Russell. *Bread and Jam for Frances.* New York: Scholastic Book Services, 1969.

Lasker, Joe. *Lentil Soup.* Chicago: Albert Whitman & Co., 1977.

Mandry, Kathy. *How to Make Elephant Bread.* New York: Pantheon Books, 1971.

Marshall, James. *Yummers.* New York: Houghton Mifflin Co., 1973.

Mayer, Mercer. *Frog Goes to Dinner.* New York: Dial Press, 1974.

McCloskey, Robert. *Blueberries for Sal.* New York: Viking Press, 1948.

McCloskey, Robert. *One Morning in Maine.* New York: Viking Press, 1952.

Patz, Nancy. *Pumpernickel Tickle and Mean Green Cheese.* New York: Franklin Watts, Inc., 1978.

Politi, Leo. *Three Stalks of Corn.* New York: Charles Scribner's Sons, 1976.

Seidler, Rosalie. *Panda Cake.* New York: Scholastic Book Services, 1978.

Sendak, Maurice. *Chicken Soup with Rice.* New York: Harper & Row, Publishers, Inc., 1962.

Seuss, Dr. *Green Eggs and Ham.* New York: Random House, Inc., 1960.

Yaffe, Alan. *The Magic Meatballs.* Illus. Karen Born Anderson. New York: Dial Press, 1979.

Sand and Water Play

Though the sand table and water table are rapidly vanishing from our primary grade classrooms, many kindergarten and preschool teachers still see the value of expressive play with sensorial materials. Literature that might be related to sand and water play includes books about the beach or bathtub and any of the dramatic play books mentioned in the next section, for any story that can be acted out can also be told with manipulatives in the sand or water table areas. The following books appear to be most directly related to sand and water.

Asche, Frank. *Sand Cake.* New York: Parents Magazine Press, 1979.

Conover, Chris. *Six Little Ducks.* New York: Thomas Y. Crowell Co., 1976.

Garelick, May. *Down to the Beach.* Illus. Barbara Cooney. New York: Scholastic Book Services, 1976.

Krasilovsky, Phyllis. *The Cow Who Fell in the Canal.* Illus. Peter Spier. Garden City, N.Y.: Doubleday & Co., Inc., 1972.

Spier, Peter. *London Bridge Is Falling Down.* Garden City, N.Y.: Doubleday & Co., Inc., 1967.

Spier, Peter. *Noah's Ark.* Garden City, N.Y.: Doubleday & Co., Inc., 1977.

Spier, Peter. *The Erie Canal.* Garden City, N.Y.: Doubleday & Co., Inc., 1970.

Dressups and Dramatization

Another traditional area in an early childhood classroom is the dressup corner. Many teachers integrate literature into the dressup corner by providing props to accompany stories. These dramatic play kits might be stored in shopping bags or in boxes labeled with each story's title and a picture. See chapter three for a detailed discussion of dramatization as a technique for involving young children with literature.

Manipulative Activities

Blocks, Legos, beads, puzzles, and the like are an integral part of early childhood classrooms. Young children enjoy building up and tearing down structures that they have created. Their manipulative activities strengthen their small muscles and improve their eye-hand coordination and visual discrimination, prerequisite skills for reading and writing.

Can literature be integrated into manipulative activities? We have found several books that might serve this purpose.

Alexander, Anne. *ABC of Cars and Trucks.* Garden City, N.Y.: Doubleday & Co., Inc., 1971.

Hutchins, Pat. *Changes, Changes.* New York: Macmillan Publishing Co., Inc., 1972.

Krahn, Fernando. *Who's Seen the Scissors?* New York: E. P. Dutton, 1975.

Spier, Peter. *London Bridge Is Falling Down.* Garden City, N.Y.: Doubleday & Co., Inc., 1967.

Ueno, Noriko. *Elephant Buttons.* New York: Harper & Row, Publishers, Inc., 1973.

There are numerous other topics that frequently become curricular areas in early childhood classrooms. Gardening, sewing, caring for a class pet—each of these and many other topics are the subjects for children's books. We don't utilize the valuable resource of children's literature nearly enough in early childhood classrooms.

Functions of Literature in the Curriculum

Once the decision is made to integrate literature into the early childhood curriculum, it is necessary to explore its functions there. What role can books play to enhance children's learning and sensitivity to a topic?

Sometimes a unit of study stems from literature. A book is read aloud and children request an activity related to the book. Often this activity leads to the use of other books on the same topic. This is the responsive approach to using literature with children.

Then there is the planned approach where the teacher has organized study around selected books. Literature might introduce a unit, be a resource throughout the unit, or be a culminating activity.

Wherever literature appears in the curriculum and for whatever reasons it is used, it is important to bear in mind the functions of literature in the curriculum. These functions include:

setting the stage for further study,

raising questions that will be explored,

putting study into a larger context,

providing secondary, representational experiences,

broadening, providing depth and background for study of a topic,

developing an atmosphere of inquiry and discovering,

establishing an atmosphere that helps children "feel" and experience the curriculum.

The functions of literature are to aid the processes by which young children learn and not simply to supply facts, preach morals, or dictate. The early childhood teacher who best understands the functions of literature has a class of children who are eager readers (or lookers at books) and who make constant references to literature. To them, literature is the core of the curriculum, always in evidence, not just an occasional experience with books.

References

Cianciolo, Patricia J. *Illustrations in Children's Books.* Dubuque, Iowa: William C. Brown Co., Publishers, 1976.

Damon, William. *The Social World of the Child.* San Francisco: Jossey-Bass Inc., Publishers, 1977.

Dreyer, Sharon S. *The Bookfinder: A Guide to Children's Literature about the Needs and Problems of Youth Aged 2-15.* Circle Pines, Minn.: American Guidance Service, 1977.

Jacob, Gale Sypher. *Independent Reading Grades One through Three: An Annotated Bibliography with Reading Levels.* Williamsport, Penn.: Bro-Dart Publishing Company, 1975.

Lamme, Linda. "Song Picture Books—A Maturing Genre of Children's Literature." *Language Arts* 56 (1979): 400-407.

Lamme, Linda, and Kane, Frances. "Children Books and Collage." *Language Arts* 53 (1976): 902-905.

6 EXAMPLES FROM THE CLASSROOM

The previous chapters of this book have provided you with the rationale for making literature an integral part of the early childhood curriculum. We have given you many suggestions. In this chapter early childhood teachers at day-care, nursery school, kindergarten, and primary grade levels share with you their experiences when using literature as a central part of the curriculum.

Gingerbread Boys, Johnny-cakes, and Buns: More Than Just Good Things to Eat

Gail E. Tompkins
McGuffey Laboratory School
Miami University
Oxford, Ohio

A gingerbread boy, a johnny-cake, and a bun are the main characters of three repetitive folktales that have delighted children around the world for generations.

The Gingerbread Boy
>Retold and illustrated by Paul Galdone
>New York: Houghton Mifflin, 1975

An old woman baked a gingerbread boy, and as she opened the oven door to take him out, he jumped out of the oven and ran out of the house and down the road. The little old woman and a little old man ran after the gingerbread boy, but they couldn't catch him. The gingerbread boy laughed and called out:

>Run! Run! Run!
>Catch me if you can!
>You can't catch me:
>I'm the Gingerbread Boy,
>I am! I am!

The gingerbread boy ran on past a cow, a horse, some men threshing wheat, and some mowers. The gingerbread boy danced and strutted; he thought that no one could catch him. Then he met a fox who gave him a ride across a river. As the water became deeper, the fox coaxed the gingerbread boy to move up onto his back, then up onto his shoulder, and finally onto his nose. When they reached the shore, the fox tipped his head and the gingerbread boy "went the way of every single gingerbread boy that ever came out of an oven."

Many other versions of this story are available. In some versions the characters who chase the gingerbread boy differ. In other versions the ending is different.

Johnny-Cake
>Retold by Joseph Jacobs
>Illustrated by Emma L. Brock
>New York: Putnam, 1967

An old woman made a Johnny-cake, and he jumped out of the oven and rolled away past a little boy, an old woman, and an old man. The Johnny-cake rolled on past two well-diggers, two ditch-diggers, a bear, and a wolf. Then Johnny-cake met a fox and boasted:

>I've outrun an old man, an old woman, and a little boy, and two well-diggers, and two ditch-diggers, a bear, and a wolf, and I can outrun you too-o-o!

The fox pretended to be hard of hearing and persuaded the Johnny-cake to come closer and closer until he was able to snatch Johnny-cake and eat him.

Another version of this story is *Johnny-cake: A Picture Book*, retold and illustrated by William Stobbs (New York: Viking, 1973).

The Bun: A Tale from Russia
   Retold and illustrated by Marcia Brown
   New York: Harcourt Brace Jovanovich, 1972

An old woman made a bun for her husband and set it on the windowsill to cool. The bun began to roll, and it rolled past the old woman and an old man and away down the road. The bun rolled past a hare, a wolf, and a bear. Then the bun met a fox and sang:

> I was scraped from the trough,
> I was swept from the bin,
> I was kneaded with cream,
> I was browned in a pan.
> By the window I cooled;
> Now five are fooled:
> I dodged the old woman,
> I fled the old man,
> I bypassed the hare,
> I slipped from the wolf,
> Brown bear couldn't stop me
> And neither can you!
> Too bad, Fox!

The fox praised the bun for his "delightful song," but explained that he didn't hear well and asked the bun to sit on his nose and sing the song again. Foolishly the bun hopped onto the fox's nose and was quickly eaten.

Story Extensions

There are striking similarities among these three folktales. The action in each story takes the form of a race in which the main character is chased by other characters. With increasing repetition of words and events, each story builds to a quick climax, the capture of the runaway main character by a crafty fox. These three tales exemplify the repetition aspect of story structure. Repetition involves both repeating words and repeating events in stories by adding new characters. Repetition is an easy stylistic device for young children to understand and use. Through a variety of activities involving these three stories, young children can investigate the repetition form and learn to incorporate it in the stories they tell and write. The activities are grouped together in six categories; however, it is suggested that the teacher do activities 1-4 with each story and then proceed to activities 5 and 6.

1. Sharing the folktales. Read the three folktales to the children, making sure to increase your reading speed to add excitement as each story reaches the climax. Encourage the children to join in repeating the main character's refrain. Collect different versions of *The Gingerbread Boy* and have the children compare the characters and the endings of the different versions. After reading the three stories, discuss the similarities among the stories.

2. Creative dramatics. Have the children take turns acting out the folktales. As the children become familiar with the words, have them join the teacher in retelling the story.

3. Retelling the stories. Have the children make a set of finger puppets to use in retelling one of the stories. The children can make finger puppets by drawing, coloring, and cutting out small pictures of the characters and then attaching the pictures to small paper rings that were cut and taped to fit the children's fingers. The children take turns retelling the folktale in small groups using their finger puppets as props. Young children are so imaginative that it is very likely that their stories will be modified as they retell them. An example is offered in figure 15, where the gingerbread boy is transformed into a gingerbread girl.

4. Cooking. Cooking activities fit naturally with these three folktales. To accompany *The Gingerbread Boy* make gingerbread cookies and have the children help to decorate them. Johnny-cakes are cornmeal pancakes. Look for a recipe on the back of a package of cornmeal. Serve johnny-cakes with butter and maple syrup. After reading *The Bun* make buns from scratch or split and heat hamburger buns. Set out cinnamon and sugar, cheese spread, or peanut butter for the children to have on their buns.

5. Creating new stories. After the children have had many experiences with the three folktales, they can use the repetition patterns in creating new stories. Use a class collaboration story to demonstrate to the children how to create new repetition stories. On the day my class composed a class story, it was just before John's birthday, and we made a story about John's runaway birthday cake. As a class we shared ideas about what would happen to the cake and the characters the cake would outrun. We even took a vote to determine how the story would end, and the children decided

The Gingerbread Girl
Story and Finger Puppets by Evelyn, Age 7

Once there was an old woman and an old man. They were very poor, and they wanted a little girl. They had a little flour, a little ginger, and a little baking soda, and so they decided to make a gingerbread girl. They put too much baking soda in it so the gingerbread girl popped out of the oven and started running.

She ran, ran, ran, ran, and she ran past a cow. The cow said, "Moo, moo. Keep running. I can catch you and you know it, too!" The gingerbread girl answered, "No, you can't. Run, run as fast as you can. You can't catch me. I'm the gingerbread girl." And so they ran and ran, and soon the cow got tired and decided to stop.

The gingerbread girl kept on running, and soon she came to a duck. And the duck said, "Quack-quack, quack-quack. I want to catch you. So stop so I can catch you." The gingerbread girl answered, "Run, run as fast as you can. You can't catch me. I'm the gingerbread girl." And so they kept running for a little while. Then the duck got tired and she stopped running by a little pond.

And then the gingerbread girl kept running until she came to a dog. The dog said, "Ruff, ruff, ruff. Stop, I want to eat you." The gingerbread girl said, "No! Run, run as fast as you can. You can't catch me. I'm the gingerbread girl." And so they ran on, and they ran on, and they ran on. Then the dog got tired and stopped.

And then she came to a cat. The cat said, "Mew, mew. Let me carry you. Your legs must be tired. Trust me, I don't want to eat you." And so the gingerbread girl hopped onto the back of the cat because her legs were tired. And they walked on a little while, and then the cat said, "My back is getting tired. Please get off." And so she did.

Then the gingerbread girl was sitting by a bush, and a cricket came out and said, "Chirp-chirp, chirp-chirp. Let me have a little bite of you." The gingerbread girl said, "No, I don't want you to eat me. Run, run as fast as you can. You can't catch me. I'm the gingerbread girl."

And so she ran on, and there was a gerbil. The gerbil said, "I've eaten many gingerbread girls, and I'm going to eat you, too." Chomp! The gerbil ate her up!

Figure 15. Child's retelling and dramatization of the story of the gingerbread boy.

that the cake would become lonely and go back to John's house in time for his birthday party. For a class story the teacher becomes the scribe and records the story on a large chart for the children. After writing the story, the children can make illustrations to add to the chart. Next the children can create their own stories. Provide the children with booklets of paper and have them draw a series of pictures to tell original repetitive stories. Later the children can add the words beside the pictures or have the teacher record their dictation. Some children's stories will very closely follow the folktales the class has read, while other children's stories will be as creative and

original as the story about a runaway pencil in figure 16.

6. Other repetition books. Here are some other picture books that use the repetition form. Try reading some of these and repeating some of the previously discussed activities with them.

Brown, Margaret W. *Home for a Bunny.* Racine, Wis.: Western Publishing Co., Inc., 1975.

Burningham, John. *Mr. Grumpy's Outing.* New York: Holt, Rinehart and Winston, Inc., 1971.

de Regniers, Beatrice S. *May I Bring a Friend?* New York: Atheneum Publishers, 1964.

Domanska, Janina. *The Turnip.* New York: Macmillan Publishing Co., Inc., 1969.

The Little Red Pencil
Story and Picture by Heather, Age 7

Once there was a girl named Heather, and she had a little red pencil. One day it got tired of being used for work all the time so it ran away. And I said, "Don't run away. I need you."

But he ran all the way to Jacqueline's desk, and she said, "Go back to Heather." And the pencil said, "No, I ran away from Heather, and I can run away from you, too."

Then he ran all the way to Kristen's desk, and she said, "Go back to Heather. She needs you." And the pencil said, "No, I ran away from Heather and Jacqueline, and I can run away from you, too."

Next he ran all the way to Michelle's desk, and she said, "Go back to Heather's desk." And the pencil said, "No, I ran away from Heather and Jacqueline, and Kristen, and I can run away from you, too."

So he ran on and on to Tiffany's desk. And she grabbed the pencil and said, "Here Heather, this is your pencil."

Figure 16. Child's original story using repetition pattern.

Ets, Marie. *Elephant in a Well.* New York: Viking Press, 1972.

Flack, Marjorie. *Ask Mister Bear.* New York: Macmillan Publishing Co., Inc., 1971.

Kroll, Steven. *The Tyrannosaurus Game.* New York: Holiday House, Inc., 1976.

Sawyer, Ruth. *Journey Cake, Ho!* New York: Viking Press, 1953.

Trees

Margaret C. Holmes
Kindergarten teacher
J. J. Finley Elementary School
Gainesville, Florida

As an ecology-minded person who also happens to teach kindergarten, I feel it is most important to make my five- and six-year-old learners aware of the wonder and beauty of nature. Too often teachers see the teaching of science for young children as strictly a first-hand approach. Then as one progresses up the grades, science teaching be-comes a text-book-only subject. So I decided to involve my children through literature with one aspect of the natural environment—trees.

My first step was to gather together as many books as I could find about trees. I searched through the local libraries and bookstores for books on trees. Then I selected the books that I felt my children would most enjoy.

The criteria I used for selecting the books to share with my students included:

1. Was the information that was in the book accurate and clear?

2. Were the illustrations in the book attractive and did they add to and correspond with the text?

3. Was the language or style of writing used in the book interesting, colorful, and rich in descriptions?

4. Could my children identify with the trees that were discussed?

5. Did the book appeal to me?

To begin the unit of study I read aloud *The Old Stump* by Hawkinson. The story revolves around an old stump in the middle of a forest and the mouse family that lives in the base of the stump. During the course of a day and night, many animals visit the stump. The story is short, lively, and finely complemented by the water color illustrations. The stump on our playground was compared to the stump in the story. A trip to the playground armed with magnifying glasses resulted in much observation, touching, discussion, and some language experience stories.

Next we read two books that follow the life cycle of an oak tree, Hutchins's *Lives of an Oak Tree* and Tresselt's *The Dead Tree*. Because of the duplication of themes, the children were able to make comparisons between the styles of writing and illustrations of the two books. Hutchins's book was accurate and clearly illustrated but rather long and a little dull in comparison with Tresselt's *The Dead Tree*, which was rich in metaphors and similies and beautifully detailed illustrations. After reading the two books, we planned a nature walk to the wooded area on the school campus. We made a list of things to look for, including acorns, leaves, "baby trees," nests, animal holes, termite tunnels, and fungus. There are several fallen trees in the woods so the children had the opportunity to see beetles, ants, and termites hard at work on the trees. Upon our return to the classroom, we checked off the things we had seen and added a few new things. Watercolor paints were available for the children to paint their impressions.

While on the nature walk, some of the children gathered leaves, pinecones, acorns, and sticks. We put them into a large box to save for further activities.

The next day I introduced the children to two reference books on trees, Zim and Martin's *Trees: A Guide to Familiar American Trees* and Rush's *The Beginning Knowledge Book of Backyard Trees*. Both books have full color, detailed pictures of leaves, seeds, and tree forms. Some children became very involved in comparing the found leaves with the pictures in the two books. Other children made crayon rubbings of the leaves, and still others made collages using the materials we had collected on our nature walk.

The next book we read about trees was *A Tree Is Nice* by Udry. This book tells, in very clear and simple terms, why a tree is nice. Simont's watercolor and wash illustrations earned the book the Caldecott Medal. After reading the book, the children colored pictures of why they liked trees and dictated sentences to go with their pictures. Then we bound the pictures together to make a picture book to add to our classroom library. And as Udry suggested, we planted a tree on campus, with the hope that the children would experience what she suggests:

> Everyday for years and YEARS you watch the little tree grow. You say to people, "I planted that tree." They wish they had one so they go home and plant a tree too.

There are other fine books and many poems on trees. I have included in the bibliography some that I came across. Literature is an ideal way to encourage in young children an appreciation for and involvement with nature. Good books should be available in school libraries, classrooms, and homes. An updated reference on good science trade books can be found annually in the spring issue of *Science and Children*.

Children's Literary References

Books

Adoff, Arnold. *Under the Early Morning Trees*. Illus. Ronald Himler. New York: E. P. Dutton, 1978.

Bulla, Clyde Robert. *A Tree Is a Plant*. Illus. Lois Lignell. New York: Thomas Y. Crowell Co., 1960.

Hawkinson, John. *The Old Stump*. Chicago: Albert Whitman & Co., 1965.

Morse, Flo. *How Does It Feel to Be a Tree?* Illus. Clyde Watson. New York: Scholastic Book Services, 1976.

Peet, Bill. *Farewell to Shady Glade*. Boston: Houghton Mifflin Co., 1966.

Rush, Hanniford. *Backyard Trees*. Illus. Raul Mina Mora. New York: Macmillan Publishing Co., Inc., 1964.

Selsam, Millicent E. *Maple Tree*. Photographs by Jerome Wexler. New York: William Morrow & Co., 1968.

Silverstein, Shel. *The Giving Tree*. New York: Harper & Row, Publishers, Inc., 1964.

Tresselt, Alvin. *The Dead Tree*. Illus. Charles Robinson. New York: Scholastic Book Services, 1972.

Udry, Janice May. *A Tree Is Nice*. Illus. Marc Simont. New York: Harper & Row, Publishers, Inc., 1956.

Zim, Herbert S., and Martin, Alexander C. *Trees: A Guide to Familiar American Trees*. Illus. Dorothea Barlowe and Sy Barlowe. New York: Golden Press, 1952.

Poems

Brewton, Sara, and Brewton, John E. *Sing a Song of Seasons*. Illus. Vera Bock. New York: Macmillan Publishing Co., Inc., 1955.

   a. Thompson, Dorothy Brown. "Arbor Day." p. 141.

  b. Behn, Harry. "Trees." p. 144.
  c. Carr, Mary Jane. "The Big Swing-Tree Is Green Again." p. 158.

Huffard, Grace T., and Carlisle, Laura M. *My Poetry Book*. New York: Holt, Rinehart and Winston, Inc., 1956.
  a. Kilmer, Joyce. "Trees." p. 266.
  b. Davies, Mary Carolyn. "Be Different to Trees." p. 269.
  c. Abbey, Henry. "What Do We Plant?" p. 269.
  d. Roberts, Elizabeth Madox. "Strange Trees." p. 278.

Untermeyer, Louis. *The Golden Treasury of Poetry*. Illus. Joan Walsh Anglund. New York: Golden Press, 1959.
  a. McCord, David. "Everytime I Climb a Tree." p. 253.
  b. Very, Jones. "The Tree."

Shoes

Rose Merenda
Kindergarten teacher
Henry Barnard Laboratory School
Rhode Island College
Providence, Rhode Island

To a young child, shoes, and especially *new* shoes, have a particular magic. The oft-repeated, "I have new shoes today" in a proud, awe-filled voice has launched many a school day, and sparked a keener look at everyone's shoes with excited conversation. In our classroom, I usually read the following poems.

New Shoes

When I am walking down the street
I do so like to watch my feet.
Perhaps you do not know the news
Mother has bought me fine new shoes!

Marjorie Seymour Watts

New Shoes

I have new shoes in the fall-time
And new ones in the spring.
Whenever I wear my new shoes
I always have to sing.

Alice Wilkins

Early in the year the children responded well to these. As our poetry collection grew, we learned and enjoyed some fun-sounding texture words by listening to the following:

New Shoes

New shoes are slippery.
Polished and trippery.
I like new shoes.
I like the black ones all aglow
From shiny heel to shiny toe.
I like the white ones, too, that feel
Velvety from toe to heel.
I like the plain brown ones to play in
Go to school and spend the day in.
I like new shoes.

Irma S. Black

Old Shoes

Old shoes are lumpy
Scratched up and bumpy.
I like old shoes.
I like the way they bend and feel
Wrinkle-y from toe to heel.
I like the way no one says "no"
When I scrape them on the toe.
I wear new shoes when I go out,
But old ones when I crawl about.
I like old shoes.

Irma S. Black

Old shoes, to my kindergarten children, were "more fun to play in, to climb trees, to get dirty, to get sand in, and felt good." Somehow they understood new shoes do not stay new for long. And, it really did not matter. The subject of shoes as a theme for learning had aroused our curiosity. Why not pursue it?

For us, children's literature facilitated the planning of in-depth multidisciplinary experiences. Storybooks made excellent turn-on agents for this teacher and her youngsters. An expansive web of resources and activities was readily spun. Reactions and responses to the stories about shoes stimulated, supported, and sustained imaginations, interests, and intellects. Step into our shoes, then, to share and to appreciate with us.

We began by reading *New Blue Shoes* by Eve Rice and thoroughly enjoyed the mother–child dialogue. Amused at Rebecca's persistence in wanting the blue shoes, we rejoiced at her decision to buy them. This was also a good time to read ffrida Wolfe's poem *Choosing Shoes*, and to compare how the book and the poem were alike and not alike. Eve Rice's illustrations, simple and precise, helped the children to organize and arrange a classroom shoe store. "Playing shoe store" was always fun but serious business. At the same time the children acquired information about the common object, shoes; expanded communication skills; increased understanding of social roles; and practiced math and logical thinking skills. Classifying, sorting, measuring, distinguishing left and right, the children gained satisfaction from their busy activity.

Our shoe store contained assorted grown-up shoes. Wearing different pairs fostered different feelings. One day I read Beatrice Schenk de Regniers's shoe interlude *What Can You Do with a Shoe?* Delightful words and illustrations (Maurice Sendak's) blended playfully and prompted the children to agree: Shoes *are* really to wear, of course. A "shoes are for" inventory elicited from the five year olds included:

tying	getting (some new ones)
jumping	keeping on
buckling	feeling good in
running	sleeping (with shoes on)
hopping	playing baseball
walking	putting on
polishing	galloping
skipping	buying

Shoes must be active, busy objects in a child's world!

Presenting and discussing the two stories *Where Is My Shoe?* and *Angela's New Shoes* helped children to relate to others like themselves. Often stories such as these provide stimulus for teaching logical thinking. Having heard *Where Is My Shoe?*, the children offered several possible solutions for how the raccoon had taken the little girl's shoe. Requesting only "shoes" for one's birthday posed a different problem in *Angela's New Shoes*. Confronting problems we ourselves create made an insightful group discussion.

As we became more involved with our shoe theme, we also learned people's shoes differ for work, play, climate, or geographical location. For sharing time, children brought wooden and other foreign shoes. With a pair of shiny red lacquered clogs in one hand, I read Masako Matsuno's *A Pair of Red Clogs*. This tale of the author's own childhood was a wonderful introduction to a foreign author and a far away country. We also made ourselves a pair of clogs or getas from cardboard and ribbon. Walking in our own getas helped us to feel one difference in shoes and in people.

Another difference, a magical one perhaps, occurred when reading *The Elves and the Shoemaker*. Elf magic in this story time favorite inspired both the creation of a cobbler shop and creative dramatization. With the materials in our cobbler shop, the five year olds intently practiced lacing, buckling, polishing, and hammering. Of these, the favorite was polishing their own shoes. Our principal came and polished his, too!

Within the framework of the cobbler shop, groups of children spontaneously dramatized the story in their own delightful, serious, but accurate way. From this, they easily moved into a larger play, integrating music, instruments, art, and math, along with storytelling. Freya Littledale's illustrated book was their reference for sequence, costumes, and staging. Everyone had a turn to take it home. Throughout, the children demonstrated that the magic mood and meaning of "doing for others" had captured them.

The color tone of several nursery rhymes that mention shoes particularly enticed the four year olds. Of course, *The Old Woman in the Shoe* was a favorite to recite, to play act, and to recreate using construction paper. The word "trousers" in *Diddle, Diddle Dumpling* fascinated them. The idea of going to bed with one shoe off and one on perplexed them. However, we cheerfully responded to the powerful rhythm in many physical ways.

Extending word power is essential as well. After reading *Cobbler, Cobbler* a few times, I explored "cobbler" with these four year olds. A cobbler, they said, is someone who:

cobbs your shoes and makes them new
fixes your shoes
is a shoemaker
is a shoe fixer
is a shoe mender

Indeed he is! All of these.

Always, Brian Wildsmith's vibrant illustrations in *Mother Goose* pleased the children. It was important to foster appreciation of the splendid artistic quality of his interpretations.

For my children and me, then, these and other storybooks, poems, and rhymes were and are important to our learning about shoes . . . old or new, real or pretend. Our collection of shoes for "Show and Tell" had grown into a classroom "Shoe Museum" to which our books were added. Our field trip downtown to visit an actual shoe store and a nearby cobbler shop had neatly laced together our school world and the real world.

Certainly we had heard, seen, and felt much in and through our stories and poems. Shoes *are* shoes, but shoes as a theme for learning in children's literature made it possible to weave a rich educational and aesthetic tapestry for my children.

Children's Book References

Stories

de Regniers, Beatrice Schenk. *What Can You Do with a Shoe?* Illus. Maurice Sendak. New York: Harper and Brothers, 1955.

Gaulke, Gloria. *Where Is My Shoe?* New York: Holt, Rinehart and Winston, Inc., 1963.

Littledale, Freya. *The Elves and the Shoemaker.* Retold and illustrated by Freya Littledale. New York: Scholastic Book Services, 1975.

Matsuno, Masako. *A Pair of Red Clogs.* New York: World Publishing Co., 1960.

Rice, Eve. *New Blue Shoes.* New York: Macmillan Publishing Co., Inc., 1975.

Snavely, Ellen. *Shoes for Angela.* New York: Follett Publishing Co., 1962.

Poems

"New Shoes" by Marjorie Seymour Watts. *More Poems to Read to the Very Young.* Selected by Josette Frank. New York: Random House, Inc., 1968.

"New Shoes" by Alice Wilkins. *Let's-Read-Together Poems.* Selected and tested by Helen A. Brown and Harry J. Heltman. New York: Row Peterson and Co., 1949.

"Old Shoes" and "New Shoes" from *Read Me More Stories.* Compiled by the Child Study Association 1949, 1977. New York: Thomas Y. Crowell Co.

"Choosing Shoes" by ffrida Wolfe. *Let's Enjoy Poetry.* Selected by Rosalind Hughes. Boston: Houghton Mifflin Co., Inc., 1958.

Fairy Tales

Sharon C. Milner
Day care teacher
Baby Gator Day Care Center
Gainesville, Florida

Young children love to hear stories read aloud. After taking a graduate class in Children's Literature I came to understand the need not only to read, but to thoroughly involve children with books. I became convinced of the educational values of fairy tales, especially in fostering healthy emotional development, after reading Bettleheim's *The Uses of Enchantment* (1977), and I re-

solved to find a way to use fairy tales as the basis for a preschool curriculum.

The curriculum at Baby Gator Day Care Center at the University of Florida centers around a weekly theme. I shared my idea of involving children with selected fairy tales with my coworkers. They were very enthusiastic, so we decided to start with "Cinderella" and plan activities for a different tale each week.

At our weekly planning meeting we discussed objectives for the children. These included:

1. a better understanding of the concepts "author" and "illustrator" through exposure to several versions of the same story;

2. integration of as many curriculum areas as possible;

3. increased storytelling ability;

4. stimulation of dramatic play based on the stories.

The next step was to brainstorm possible activities. These are listed below. All were implemented and were a huge success based on the level of involvement of the children. This model could be used for other fairy tales and for involving children with literature in general.

"Cinderella"

Books:

Galdone, Paul. *Cinderella.* McGraw-Hill, 1978.

Perrault, Charles. *Cinderella or The Little Glass Slipper,* illustrated by Marcia Brown. Patterson, N.J.: Charles Scribner's Sons, 1954.

Walt Disney version of *Cinderella.*

The books were read at separate story sessions. Children were encouraged to discuss the stories and to find similarities and differences in the versions.

Children participated in the following activities:

1. Construction of a castle and coach with large packing boxes. The children helped make and paint these objects.

2. Acting out the story in small groups, so the children had turns to play different parts.

3. Making and decorating crowns for Cinderella and the prince.

4. Baking tarts for the "ball."

5. Dancing with scarves to music.

6. Making a language experience chart about Cinderella. The teacher simply asked the children to tell her what happened in the story. The teacher wrote down whatever the child said.

7. "The Ball" consisted of makeup, costumes, music, dancing, and refreshments.

8. Taking children to see the play "Cinderella" at the local community college. The children really paid attention and enjoyed it because they knew the story.

9. Pictures were taken of all these activities and a book was made for the children.

"Snow White"

Books:

Grimm, Jacob. *Snow White and the Seven Dwarfs.* Illustrated by Wanda Gág, New York: Coward-McCann, 1938.

Grimm, Jacob. *Snow White.* Illustrated by Trina Schart Hyman, translated by Paul Heins; Little, Brown & Co., 1974.

Walt Disney version of *Snow White.*

The castle was changed into the house of the seven dwarfs. A forest made of cardboard trees with real leaves (collected on a nature walk) surrounded the cottage. Other activities included:

1. Construction of one large and one small magic mirror. Heavy duty aluminum foil was placed over styrofoam plates. The children colored faces on the mirrors with markers.

2. A bed for Snow White was made by turning the water table upside down. The children made flowers out of colored tissue paper to surround the bed.

3. "Poison apples" were made by dipping apples on sticks into honey and rolling them into a mixture of wheat germ and nuts. The recipe for the apples was made with pictures as symbols so the children could read the directions.

4. Finger puppets were made with construction paper and markers. The teacher and children cut out the shapes of the characters. The children colored them in. They were fastened like a ring to fit on the fingers.

5. A language experience chart was made in response to the teacher's statement, "Tell me about Snow White."

6. Pictures were taken and a book was made.

7. Costumes were put in the dress-up corner so the children could dress for their parts.

"Little Red Riding Hood"

Book:

Galdone, Paul. *Little Red Riding Hood.* McGraw-Hill, 1974.

The dwarfs' cottage became Grandma's house. The children helped the teachers sew several red capes. Children chose from these activities:

1. Acting out the story taking turns.

2. Tape-recording each child's version of the story.

3. Making fruit salad to take to Grandma.

4. Making paper bag puppets and a stage so children could act out the story on their own.

5. Making characters out of pellon and markers, and leaving them by the flannelboard for the children to use.

Children can benefit greatly from a systematic program of involvement activities based on popular fairy tales. This project demonstrates that with motivation and creativity teachers can help children "live" these stories in an exciting and educational way.

Professional Reading

Abrahamson, Richard F. "Children's Literature Scholarship: Implications of Favat's *Child and Tale.*" *Language Arts* 55 (1978): 502-4.

Arthur, Anthony. "The Uses of Bettelheim's *The Uses of Enchantment.*" *Language Arts* 55 (1978): 455-59.

Bettelheim, Bruno. *The Uses of Enchantment: The Meaning and Importance of Fairy Tales.* New York: Random House, Inc., 1977.

Bettelheim, Bruno. "The Importance of Fairy Tales." *Instructor* 86 (1976): 79-80.

Favat, F. André. *Child and Tale: The Origins of Interest.* Urbana, Ill.: National Council of Teachers of English, 1977.

Guthrie, John T. "Research Views: Fantasy as Purpose." *The Reading Teacher* 32 (1978): 106-108.

Huck, Charlotte S. *Children's Literature in the Elementary School.* New York: Holt, Rinehart and Winston, Inc., 1979. 3rd ed.

O'Donnell, Holly O. " 'Once Upon a Time' in the Classroom." *Language Arts* 55 (1978): 534-37.

Salz, Eli, and Johnson, James. "Training for Thematic-Fantasy Play in Culturally Disadvantaged Children: Preliminary Results." 1973, ERIC No. ED 086334.

Yolen, Jane. "Shape Shifters: Every Child's Adventures in Fairy Tales." *Language Arts* 55 (1978): 699-703.

Storytelling with Flannelboards

Patricia T. Carmean
Kindergarten teacher
Heritage Christian School
Gainesville, Florida

Preschool children develop vocabulary and language skills largely through imitation. What better method to expand these skills than through the method of storytelling? When children have the opportunity to hear a large repertoire of stories in their early years, it will increase their appreciation of literature.

Storytime is a daily activity in my kindergarten classroom. My goal is to encourage the children to begin telling their own stories. I begin by introducing wordless books (books with pictures but no printed story lines). When introducing a wordless book, I share the book with the children while asking for their comments. These comments are written down and the story is read again (Cullinan and Carmichael, *Literature and Young Children*, NCTE, 1978).

There are many techniques of storytelling. Children at approximately age five enjoy having something to manipulate. Therefore, one of the most popular styles of storytelling at this age uses flannelboards. Flannelboards are inexpensive and easy to make. One of the most economical ways is to use an old receiving blanket for the flannel and staple it to corrugated cardboard. This board would be lightweight and easy for a child to maneuver.

Felt, pellon, and tagboard make suitable figures for the flannelboard. If tagboard is used, a strip of sandpaper or velcro can be attached in order for the figures to adhere to the board. Figures can be traced from picture books or coloring books or drawn freehand.

When using the method of flannelgraph in telling stories, I try to know the story well. I practice reading it over and over. I don't memorize, but I do retain key phrases and sequence. I place the figures close at hand and practice placing them on the board and removing them at appropriate intervals during the story. When I am ready to present the story to the children, I tell the story and manipulate the pieces myself. Then I repeat the story (or play a tape recording of it) the following day with children manipulating the pieces. The next time we do the story, the children help tell it. As the different children help tell the story and recall the events in sequence, they take turns putting up the various story character pieces. With the teacher close by, children gain the confidence that they might lack if trying to attempt a story on their own.

When selecting stories, I choose those that appeal to children at kindergarten age level. Some of the popular stories I used in my classroom were *The Gingerbread Boy, Henny Penny,* and *Three Billy Goats Gruff.* On occasion, I made up stories that were prompted by situations in the classroom. In one instance the story was about a bear cub who was kind and helpful, always doing things for other people. This was used to motivate children to help their classmates.

After telling a story, I leave the figures in a folder close to the flannelboard so that children can use them later in the day. You might make a cassette tape of the story to put in a listening center where the children can follow along in the book as they learn the story. Or, if it is a longer story, place the tape recorder by the flannelboard for the children to play as they manipulate the pieces. When a cassette player is placed near the flannelboard, children can record themselves telling stories, and then play it back for themselves and others.

The children enjoyed manipulating the figures and repeating phrases of the story that they recalled. As this became a familiar activity, the children expanded on stories they had heard, showing their own imagination. This activity demonstrated to the children that storytelling is a pleasurable and acceptable activity. Through such shared activities the children began to develop confidence in speaking before a group, and they learned to express their thoughts clearly.

After the introductory day, the flannel file folder (along with an identifying picture on the outside—gingerbread man, etc.) was put into a decorated cardboard box. This cardboard box can more appropriately be called the "story box," for it can hold a wealth of figures to stimulate a child's creative mind. It was stored in a prominent place that was accessible to the children.

The desire to tell stories should come from the child and not be required of the child by a teacher or other adult. The stories the children especially enjoy will be retold often.

After children have experienced telling stories with a flannelboard, it will not be long before they will want to make some figures to accompany their own stories. Simple figures can be made from paper and backed with flannel. Crayons or, preferably, magic markers can be used to color the pictures.

After having heard stories in school, a kindergarten child in my classroom began improvising stories at home. At first she took a doll stroller and put a receiving blanket over it to make it look like a flannelboard. She used paper figures from Sunday School, or those she cut out of magazines, for her story characters. She copied stories that she had heard, first telling them to her imaginary friends and then later to her younger sister. When she had her sister as an audience, her storytelling intensified.

I then suggested that the parent make a "real" flannelboard for her child. After the flannelboard was made, it became the center of attention. When the parent saw the excitement generated by the board, she became involved in making felt figures to use on the board. She made mommy, daddy, baby, trees, a house, a cat, a dog, etc.— what she thought of generally as a family. Later she made up items from her daughter's suggestions.

The older daughter started using the board and figures, telling familiar stories in her own way to her younger sister. The children immediately made up stories on their own. In the beginning the younger sister would simply put up each figure and name it, but later her stories started to emerge with a beginning, a middle, and an ending.

Storytelling has become a fun activity in this child's home. They like to tell stories to one another, and then take turns being the teller or the listener. They also share ideas with other members of the family including mommy, daddy, grandma, grandpa, or anyone whose attention they can capture for a few minutes.

Making flannelgraphs can, therefore, become a parent involvement activity. Simple instructions can be sent home on a ditto, or a flannelboard-making workshop could be held. This would be an ideal time to offer ideas on how to tell flannelboard stories.

Once a teacher has collected and stored a wide range of flannel stories, a system for "checking out" a flannelboard and a box of story figures could be set up. Then children could practice telling their stories to parents, grandparents, and younger brothers or sisters. This would be an excellent way to foster the language development of a younger sibling. Another idea would be to have a parent party once a month where, in addition to other things, students could perform their flannelboard stories.

List of Books Suitable for Flannelboard Stories

Anderson, Paul S. *Storytelling with the Flannel Board, Book One*. Minneapolis: T. S. Denison & Co., Inc., 1974.

Anderson, Paul S. *Storytelling with the Flannel Board, Book Two*. Minneapolis: T. S. Denison & Co., Inc., 1974.

de Paola, Tomie. *Pancakes for Breakfast*. New York: Harcourt Brace Jovanovich, Inc., 1978.

Galdone, Paul. *The Three Billy Goats Gruff*. New York: Houghton Mifflin Co., 1973.

Galdone, Paul. *The Horse, the Fox, and the Lion*. Adapted from *The Fox and the Horse* by the Brothers Grimm. New York: Houghton Mifflin Co., 1968.

Galdone, Paul. *The Gingerbread Boy*. New York: Houghton Mifflin Co., 1975.

Galdone, Paul. *The Monkey and the Crocodile (A Jataka Tale from India)*. New York: Houghton Mifflin Co., 1969.

The Rand McNally Book of Favorite Read-Aloud Stories. Chicago: Rand McNally & Co., 1959.

Roy, Ron. *Three Ducks Went Wandering*. New York: Houghton Mifflin Co., 1979.

The Three Bears and Fifteen Other Stories. Selected and illustrated by Anne Rockwell. New York: Thomas Y. Crowell Co., 1975.

Humor

Charlotte A. Beckham
Second grade teacher
Shell Elementary School
Hawthorne, Florida

Children rate humorous stories high among preferred reading (Hawkins, 1978). Humor theorists seem to agree that humor is developmental, but have not settled on the cognitive factors that influence it or the age levels at which they are operating.

Hawkins includes four categories of humor in children's literature.

1. Verbal: the manipulation of language, such as play on words, puns, jokes, sarcasm.

2. Human Predicament: a situation in which either oneself or someone else appears foolish or suffering from momentary misfortune.

3. Absurdity: ridiculous humor lacking reason, including the preposterous and slapstick.

4. Incongruity: a more subtle kind of humor that associates recognized incompatibles, relying on illogical relationships between people, objects, or ideas and their environment.

Appreciation for different types of humor varies according to chronological age. Children's preference for verbal humor increases with age. Young children seem to prefer absurd humor (Hawkins, 1978).

My second grade class and I greatly enjoyed our collection and study of funny books. We gathered the books from our school library, public library, home collections, and our own classroom books. We set out to read and become involved with as many humorous books as possible. Often our greatest enjoyment came from the story and illustration alone. But at other times we became more involved with the book. Some examples follow.

Art activities can be used to enhance story comprehension. By taking the main idea and using our own illustrations, we developed comprehension accuracy. These activities included drawing with crayon, chalk, paint, or magic marker. Projects were done individually and in small groups. For more elaborate creations, clay, paper-mache, cloth, and other materials were used.

For many humorous books, the excellent illustrations are as funny as the story. Even though we enjoy good illustrations, books without them provide a greater creative experience. An opportunity to use a book as a model for our own illustrations was provided by *Animals Should Definitely Not Wear Clothing* by Judi Barrett. This book is full of troubles that plague animals wearing clothes. The children were given the task of creating their own animal dilemmas using crayons, chalk, or markers. They came up with an octopus having trouble keeping on gloves, an elephant's too-tight dress, and many others. We took these individual illustrations, wrote a few lines to join them, and compiled our own classroom books.

Language experience activities seem to be a joy for the children when incorporated within a lighthearted story. The initial activity is reading the story, either silently or aloud. Listening to a story being read aloud is good practice for listening skills, as well as a positive literature experience. Language involvement can be both written and spoken with our funny books. The children can read the story and then, in small groups, retell the story to their peers. This requires both comprehension of the story and skills for expressing thoughts. These concepts, hidden within an assignment using a funny book, seem to magically change into a fun-filled privilege rather than another job to do.

A similar procedure is to read a funny book and then write a different ending, version, or summary of it. Our special book for this activity was *Hubert's Hair-Raising Adventure* by Bill Peet. Hubert, the haughty lion, burned his mane by accident. The other animals help with a cure of crocodile tears that cause his mane to grow and grow—all over everywhere. The children fell in love with this excellent book. After many readings, aloud and silently, we decided to help Hubert with our own magic mane-growing cures. Thus, a creative writing assignment was concealed within a fun-filled task. The children had a great time. Their cures included magic shampoo, fish scales, prune juice, etc. Their stories ranged in length from a paragraph to two pages.

Dramatic expression is enhanced by funny books. These activities can range from simple, short role playing to skits and plays. We found a book that was ideal for short role playing, *Down in the Boondocks* by Wilson Gage. This story relates in rhyme what happens when a thief decides to rob a deaf farmer. The story centers on noises and the deaf farmer's funny experiences. The children acted out parts of the story such as the squeaky wagon, the wife yelling at the poor farmer so he can hear her, etc. The rhyme and repetition allowed the other children to chime in at times in a choral speaking manner.

Using involvement activities with a funny book is no different than using them with any other literature form. Funny stories seem to make any activity more relaxed, enjoyable, and productive. Ideas for story involvement seem to be hidden within each book, ready to jump out at you at any time. This flexibility from routine appeals to young children. It provides great learning and enjoyment.

We have included a list of some of our favorite funny books for you to enjoy and use. Our list of funny books is still growing.

Absurdity Humor

Allard, Harry. *The Stupids Step Out.* Boston: Houghton Mifflin Co., 1974.
The Stupid family and their dog, Kitty, have a fun-filled day doing ridiculous things.

Barrett, Judith. *Animals Should Definitely Not Wear Clothing.* New York: Atheneum Publishers, 1970.
If animals did wear clothing like we do, they just might get into a lot of trouble. This book is full of their troubles.

Hewett, Anita. *Mrs. Mopple's Washing Line.* New York: McGraw-Hill Book Co., 1966.
The wind plays an awful trick on Mrs. Mopple when it blows her wash off the line to some very strange places.

McPhail, David. *The Bear's Toothache.* Boston: Little, Brown & Co., 1972.
A young boy helps a bear overcome his toothache.

Parish, Peggy. *Good Work, Amelia Bedelia.* New York: Greenwillow Books, 1976.
Literal-minded Amelia Bedelia, the housekeeper, carries out her list of chores in an upside down fashion.

Peet, Bill. *Chester the Worldly Pig.* Boston: Houghton Mifflin Co., 1965.
Chester was unhappy being a plain pig. He'd rather be a circus star.

Peet, Bill. *How Droofus the Dragon Lost His Head.* Boston: Houghton Mifflin Co., 1971.
Droofus lives on a farm with a little boy. He gets into a most comical situation while helping the king.

Peet, Bill. *The Spooky Tail of Prewitt Peacock.* Boston: Houghton Mifflin Co., 1973.
Prewitt has trouble with his tail feathers. Instead of their being beautiful, their design forms a spooky face.

Peet, Bill. *Whingdingdilly.* Boston: Houghton Mifflin Co., 1970.
Scamp is tired of being a plain dog, so Zildy the witch zaps him into a mixture of various animals—a whingdingdilly.

Stone, Rosetta. *Because the Bug Went Ka-choo!* New York: Random House, Inc., 1975.
The mere sneeze of a bug triggers a chain reaction involving, among others, cows, turtles, policemen, and an entire parade.

Williamson, Jane. *The Trouble with Alaric.* New York: Farrar, Straus & Giroux, Inc., 1975.
Alaric doesn't want to be a dog; he wants to be a person. Soon he discovers that being a person isn't the treat he thought it would be.

Human Predicament Humor

Berenstain, Stan, and Berenstain, Jan. *The Bears' Picnic.* New York: Random House, Inc., 1966.
Papa bear takes his family on another comical adventure, a picnic.

Gackenbach, Dick. *Hound and Bear.* New York: Houghton Mifflin Co., 1976.
Hound and Bear are very good friends until Hound plays one practical joke too many on Bear.

Gage, Wilson. *Squash Pie.* New York: Greenwillow Books, 1976.
Someone kept stealing the farmer's squash so he couldn't make squash pie.

Lobel, Arnold. *A Treeful of Pigs.* New York: Greenwillow Books, 1979.
A farmer's wife uses drastic measures to get her husband to abandon his lazy ways.

Mayer, Mercer. *Liza Lou and the Yeller Belly Swamp.* New York: Scholastic Book Services, 1976.
With her quick thinking, Liza Lou manages to outwit all the haunts, gobbly gooks, witches, and devils in the Yeller Belly Swamp.

Meyers, Bernice. *Not This Bear!* New York: Scholastic Book Services, 1971.
Dressed in a furry hat and coat, little Herman looks just like a bear. He is mistaken by a bear family for "Cousin Julius."

Peet, Bill. *The Wump World.* Boston: Houghton Mifflin Co., 1970.
The peaceful wumps, small animals, lived in their grassy, clean wump world until the Pollutians from the planet Pollutus came and polluted their world.

Slobodkina, Esphyr. *Caps for Sale.* Reading, Mass.: Addison-Wesley Publishing Co., Inc., 1947.
A cap peddler has trouble with monkeys taking his caps.

Spier, Peter. *Oh, Were They Ever Happy!* New York: Doubleday & Co., Inc., 1978.
One Saturday morning while their parents are away, the three Noonan children decide to paint the house. What a mess!

Waber, Bernard. *Ira Sleeps Over.* Boston: Houghton Mifflin Co., 1972.
Ira's first invitation to spend the night with his friend causes a problem. He can't decide whether to take his Teddy Bear or leave it at home.

Verbal Humor

Gage, Wilson. *Down in the Boondocks.* New York: Greenwillow Books, 1977.
Relates in rhyme what happens when a thief decides to rob a deaf farmer.

Peet, Bill. *Hubert's Hair-Raising Adventure.* Boston: Houghton Mifflin Co., 1959.
Hubert, the haughty lion, burned his mane by accident. The animals help with a cure of crocodile tears that cause his mane to grow and grow—all over everywhere.

Ressner, Phil. *August Explains.* New York: Harper & Row, Publishers, Inc., 1963.
August, an old wise bear, explains to young Ted bear what it would be like to be a little boy. Comical descriptions and illustrations from the little bear's imagination.

Reference

Hawkins, Karla J. "Elementary School Children's Preference for Selected Elements of Humor in Children's Books." Speech delivered at the Annual Convention of the National Council of Teachers of English, Kansas City, Kansas, 1978.

Weather

Elizabeth L. Worsham
Third grade teacher
Prairie View Elementary
Gainesville, Florida

Trade books can be of great benefit to a teacher who is attempting to supplement a curriculum area such as science. I found trade books to be of immeasurable value with my third-grade class because the majority of my students had difficulty reading and comprehending the third-grade science text. This meant that motivation for science and interest in science activities was at an all-time low. I decided to review my situation.

The students in my class represent a wide range of abilities. At the beginning of the year, 69% were reading below grade level. Of those below grade level, 55% were reading a full year below grade level, and 27% were reading a year-and-a-half below grade level. Also, during the year the school population fluctuates, which affects reading groups and curriculum areas. This instability is also influenced by the assignment and/or reassignment of children in various Exceptional Student Educational Programs. Consequently, many of my students were not good auditory learners. Their attention spans were limited and they had trouble sitting still.

However, this group has several positive attributes. Even though the majority of them test low on reading skills, all students enjoy Silent Sustained Reading. I try to have two fifteen-minute sessions a week. All the children are enthusiastic about finding a book and reading during this

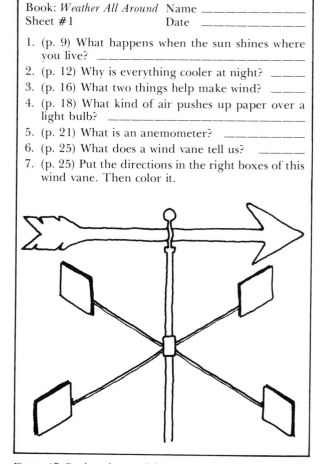

Figure 17. Book review worksheet.

time, and they are also very interested in learning and completing assignments.

Using this information, I thought about different ways I could supplement the school text for my science unit on weather. In the school library I found a very good selection of trade books on weather, ranging from easy reading to difficult. The four books I found most useful were:

Kinney, Jean, and Kinney, Cle. *What Does the Cloud Do?* Young Scott Books, 1967.

Pine, Tillie S., and Levine, Joseph. *Weather All Around.* McGraw-Hill Book Co., 1966.

Polgreen, John, and Polgreen, Cathy. *Thunder and Lightening.* Doubleday & Co., Inc., 1963.

Tannehill, Ivan Ray. *All about the Weather.* Random House, Inc., 1953.

I decided to correlate the books with some teacher-made worksheets and make them easily accessible to the students. The questions were listed by page in the order they could be found in the book. I hoped in this way to interest students in actually reading the book instead of merely flipping back and forth searching for answers. A sample worksheet is given in figure 17.

I started my science "center" with four books. Each book had at least one worksheet and one of the longer books had two. Worksheets were placed in labelled manila folders near the appropriate books. I put the following directions on the wall:

"Science Smarties"

1. Choose a book.

2. Find the folder with the same name.

3. Look for page number clues to find the answers.

After using these materials for several weeks, I gave my students an opportunity to comment on this procedure by filling out the following questionnaire:

Science

1. Did you go to the science table and do a worksheet?   Yes   No

2. How many worksheets did you do?   _____

3. Do you like to be able to find the answers without the teacher reading to you?
Yes   Maybe   No

4. Do you want science worksheets for our unit on animals?   Yes   No

5. Do you like having books in the room from the library about what we are studying?   Yes   No

6. If so, why do you like having books in the room about the things we study?
_____

In response to question number six, Annie said, "Because when I am done [with my work] I can get one and study and the pictures are good." Mary said, "I just like to read the books cause it learn me more." Mike said, "I like to read them because they are good." Tom didn't agree. He said, "I don't like to have library books!"

It took me only three hours one afternoon to set up and organize this program. For those three hours I feel that my students increased their interests in science, literature, and school!

Sharing *Anansi the Spider*

Elise Nucci
Third grade teacher
Prince George's County Schools
Maryland

Anansi the Spider is adapted from the Ashanti folktale and illustrated by Gerald McDermott (New York: Holt, Rinehart and Winston, Inc., 1976). Anansi is a vain and foolish spider who is constantly getting into trouble. Fortunately, he has six very wise sons who are both talented and resourceful. Anansi's sons are kept busy rescuing him from his predicaments, but in this story all six sons are needed when Anansi is swallowed by a fish.

Sharing the Book with K-1 Students

Share the book *Anansi the Spider* by reading the text slowly while enjoying the illustrations with the children. This introduction is a sensory approach, not an analysis!

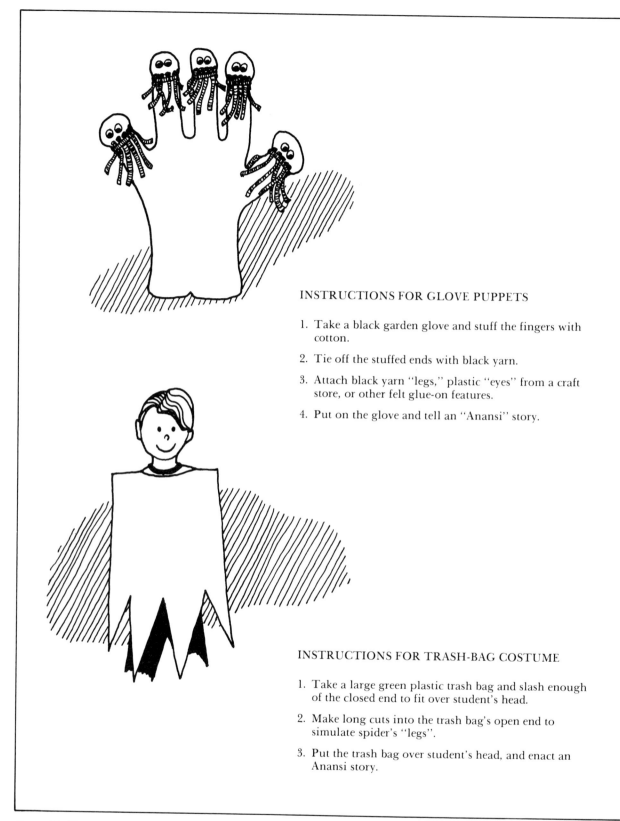

INSTRUCTIONS FOR GLOVE PUPPETS

1. Take a black garden glove and stuff the fingers with cotton.

2. Tie off the stuffed ends with black yarn.

3. Attach black yarn "legs," plastic "eyes" from a craft store, or other felt glue-on features.

4. Put on the glove and tell an "Anansi" story.

INSTRUCTIONS FOR TRASH-BAG COSTUME

1. Take a large green plastic trash bag and slash enough of the closed end to fit over student's head.

2. Make long cuts into the trash bag's open end to simulate spider's "legs".

3. Put the trash bag over student's head, and enact an Anansi story.

Figure 18. Glove puppets and trash-bag costumes.

1. Talk about: Colors (magenta, turquoise, and other unusual ones); spiders (what they look like; number of legs; their webs); and Africa (where it is; the climate). Encourage verbalizing information children already have.

2. Do an experience story: "Anansi the Spider reminds me of . . ."; "If I had crayons to color Anansi the Spider, I would choose . . . ."

3. Make Anansi's family with black felt and yarn; stuff bodies with cotton and hang the finished products in windows or from the ceiling.

4. Name Anansi's children (Cushion, etc.). Then add children, grandchildren, nieces, and nephews and "name" them according to their talents or work.

5. Invite a storyteller (grio) to come in African garments and tell additional Anansi stories.

Sharing the Book with Grades 2 and 3

There are a host of activities the teacher can use at this level to extend students' experience with this and other stories. They progress in complexity from discussion of colors to creative dramatics to bookmaking. The teacher is best qualified to pick and choose according to each group's interests and abilities.

1. Prepare a color analysis. Have students describe the feelings they have from different colors. What colors make people feel hot or cold? Sleepy or lively? Survey the group and make a poster/collage for each emotion.

2. Plan a "What if . . ." story, such as, "What if Anansi met Charlotte?" (from *Charlotte's Web*).

3. Make puppets of Anansi using old black gloves (see fig. 18). Prepare a puppet show for presentation to other groups.

4. Make trash-bag costumes from plastic trash bags, cutting strips to indicate spider legs (see fig. 18). Do improvisational role play of Anansi, his wife, and his children in a typical predicament.

5. Write an Anansi the Spider Joke Book using the popular "elephant joke" format.

6. Write a group story about Anansi and his children.

The last two suggestions can form the basis for a project that will not only extend the story and encourage creativity, but will provide students with a basic introduction to the art of bookmaking. It is important that the teacher become familiar with some of the terminology and procedures for making a book. Some useful references, which are also appropriate to give to students at this level, are *Pencil to Press: How This Book Came to Be* by Marjorie Spector (New York: Lothrop, Lee & Shepard, 1975) and *Print a Book*, written and illustrated by Heinz Kurth (Middlesex, England: Puffin Books, 1975). Also, several excellent films are available from Weston Woods Studios (389 Newton Turnpike, Weston, CT 06883).

Introduce the class to the idea of making a book by emphasizing the aspect of illustrating.

1. Show the sound filmstrip *The Preparation of a Graphic* (Weston Woods) in which Gerald McDermott describes and demonstrates his unique art style.

2. Show the sound filmstrip *Anansi the Spider* (Weston Woods), pausing on frames to discuss the applications of McDermott's artistic techniques (i.e., geometric shapes, colors, etc.).

3. If you have not already done so, suggest creating a group story in the folktale tradition. Use the overhead projector, offer the phrase "Once there was . . ." and elicit the story from the group.

4. When the story is written, form groups to sketch the major characters in the story. (Resource: Ed Emberly's *Drawing Book of Faces*)

5. When each group has decided on a composite sketch of the major characters, the drawings are presented to the entire class to sketch. (This brings unity and consistency to the illustrations.)

6. Give a simple explanation of how a book is put together by handing out a list of vocabulary and discussing each term's definition and place in the bookmaking process. Showing pictures from reference books as well as examples from a local print shop will help students see how all the pieces fit. Suggestions for a vocabulary list include:

rough manuscript	press sheets
typed manuscript	folded and gathered
galleys	pages (f and g's)
dummy	finished book
page proofs	book jacket

Additional terms referring to specific parts of a finished book should be discussed. Students could locate these elements in any book on their desks.

Title page	Dedication
(and half-title page)	Index
Copyright page	End papers
Table of Contents	

7. Prepare copy for the title page, contents, etc. for the group story.

8. Decide how much text should go on each page. Then assign individuals or groups specific pages to prepare, including a dummy for approval and a finished product. When all the text and illustrations have been assembled, the books are ready for binding.

9. When children take the time to refine their writings and drawings, the least we can do is help them make a permanent binding for their production. Books bound with yarn and construction paper don't last very long. Make the pages out of very sturdy paper or oak tag. Either take the book to a copy center and have a spiral binding made for it (be sure to allot space for margins) or bind in the following fashion:

   a. Sew the inside pages together with a sewing machine or staple them together. Ac-tually, it is better if pages are long pieces of paper folded at the center and stitched together.

   b. Make the cover by cutting two pieces of sturdy cardboard just larger than the inside pages.

   c. Tape the cardboard together at the binding with cloth tape (*not* masking tape) leaving at least ½" of space between the pieces for the back binding.

   d. Cut contact paper or fabric larger than the entire cover. Wrap it around the cardboard to make an outer cover. Using cloth tape or plastic tape, tape the first page to the front cover and the last page to the back cover. Or, to give the book a more finished appearance, use fabric or heavy paper to form end papers.

The last step is the best: read, share, and enjoy!

Additional Film Resources

Evaluation of a Graphic Concept: The Stonecutter. Weston Woods Signature Collection, Gerald McDermott. SF 454C, $30.00.

How a Picture Book Is Made. Weston Woods Signature Collection, Gerald McDermott and Steven Kellogg. SF 451C, $30.00.

7 PARENTS, VOLUNTEERS, AND AIDES: HUMAN RESOURCES FOR A LITERATURE PROGRAM

Linda Leonard Lamme
University of Florida

To help youngsters appreciate and comprehend literature most effectively, and to provide lots of "stretching" extension opportunities, you need to utilize many resources, both human and media. One adult simply can't give a group of young children all of the one-to-one attention that the acquisition of prereading and beginning reading skills and the love of literature requires. Nor can one classroom teacher provide the close, warm, physical encounters that surround the lap reading experience. Also, since more and more parents work, and since more children are growing up in one-parent families, less time is available at home for one-to-one experiences with books, writing, playing with manipulative letters, cooking, and all the other experiences that expose young children to printed language. Therefore, more of these types of experiences need to be provided at school, where many teachers rely on the help of volunteers and paraprofessionals.

Professionals

Within your own school or center there are professionals who very likely could contribute to your literature program, either on a volunteer basis or as part of their jobs. Survey your entire staff. Find out who can sing, play a musical instrument, draw, and tell stories. Exchange your talents with those of another teacher who might put variety into your class's literature curriculum. This way children in the school or center benefit from the skills and abilities of many staff members. As an added benefit, the school personnel can become closer, more like a family. One teacher might sing songs from children's books with your class while you read aloud to that teacher's class.

The school librarian is probably the most important human resource for your literature program. The librarian is likely to be a skilled oral reader and storyteller. He or she is familiar with a variety of new books that most teachers don't take the time to monitor. While visits to the library/media center should be regularly scheduled, one might also invite the librarian into the classroom on a regular basis. If you stay in the room when the librarian visits, you might pick up some tips on reading aloud or storytelling by observing the librarian. Also, librarians are usually willing to help you find and borrow books for topics of study and for individual children. In one school, each teacher gives the librarian unit topics two weeks before the start of the unit and the librarian holds back books on that topic from circulation for the exclusive use of that class.

Another professional often willing to help is a nearby university professor of children's literature, elementary education, or early childhood education. Often you can earn inservice points or university or college credits for upgrading your literature program. You might attempt such projects as improving your skill as an oral reader or storyteller, providing puppetry or dramatization opportunities for your class, extending your knowledge of children's books and media, or developing a parent program. These professionals are often sources for recent bibliographies and/or teaching ideas. Sometimes an intern or children's literature student will be assigned to a classroom to experiment with literature ideas.

Aides and Volunteers

Aides and volunteers can help to provide a program that will meet the needs of children in a class of nursery or primary age children. However, using aides or volunteers requires background and skills in peer management that may be a new challenge not covered in the previous training of most early childhood teachers. The following are some simple suggestions and guidelines for using others to enrich your classroom.

If you are fortunate enough to teach in a school that hires aides to help you, you have a head start. But even if you have an aide, you will probably want to recruit some volunteers.

What Can Aides and Volunteers Do?

The first step in using aides and volunteers is to make a list of activities that you do currently or would like to do, but that someone else could do for you. Such a list might look like this:

> read lap stories to individual children
> act as scribes taking dictation from children
> gather more books for the classroom library
> make props for drama kits to accompany stories
> make a puppet theatre and puppets for a folktale
> find some good books on "bugs"
> make a feltboard
> make feltboard characters for a story
> listen to some beginning readers read aloud
> read aloud to a small group of children
> take five children to the library/media center
> make some bookshelves
> repair old books
> organize a fundraiser to buy books or to establish a RIF program (described later in this chapter)
> tape-record individual children telling stories

Any of the activities mentioned in chapter three might be done with an aide or volunteer.

Then go back over your list and determine which tasks are ongoing, requiring regular, reliable weekly or daily assistance, and which are short projects, allowing volunteers to work on their own at night or on weekends. Sometimes working with one child is less threatening for a parent or senior citizen who has not recently been in an early childhood classroom than working with a group might be. Since many children get little positive one-to-one attention with books at home, getting volunteers for individual work is very important.

Another type of volunteer is the guest speaker. Working parents are more likely to be able to share their hobbies or careers than to be regular volunteers. A simple questionnaire might uncover a number of willing guests. Integrating their expertise into your literature curriculum by finding books and magazines on these topics greatly enhances learning on these special occasions. For every guest speaker or field trip, the children should have lots of reading, writing, listening, and talking experiences to expand their learning.

For the parent who works full time there are innumerable things that might be done at home or on weekends to support the literature program. Mary Siders, a teacher at P. K. Yonge Lab School at the University of Florida, has parents sign up for committees at the beginning of each school year. She makes it clear to the parents that it is their classroom, not just hers. Parents sign up for the construction committee, the fund-raising committee, the classroom volunteer committee, the instructional resource committee, the transportation committee, the refreshment committee, etc.

Teachers who use this approach find parents who will donate a Saturday to build things for the classroom, such as bookshelves, a reading loft, a puppet theatre, flannelboards and characters, or props for dramatic play to accompany stories. All these enhance a literature program and at the same time create the feeling of "our" classroom. Participants (builders and children as well) have a picnic lunch together and develop a happy esprit de corps.

Teachers often are without funds to do the things they would like to do with young children. A good literature curriculum needs many, many children's books. Books are expensive. A resourceful teacher will find many inexpensive ways to add to the classroom library, but even inexpensive ways need finding. A good literature curriculum involves young children with books in a variety of ways. Props, flannelboard characters, dress-ups, puppets, materials to make books—all these supplementary materials can be costly. Some parents who don't have the time or interest to do classroom volunteer work will gladly volunteer to run fund-raising activities such as garage sales, car washes, and bake sales. Parent groups are frequently the sponsors of RIF (Reading Is Fundamental) programs that, with federal subsidies, distribute free books to classes of young children.

Some parents who work full time might be willing to make things for your classroom at night or on weekends. Mary Siders has a parent folder hung by the side of her classroom door. In it are directions for her "instructional resource committee" to make things she needs in her classroom. Given clear directions and patterns, parents could make puppets, props, flannelboard characters, games, learning center tapes of stories, and other materials for the literature program. Young children are eager to demonstrate the game that their family made at home for the classroom.

There are many ways a resourceful teacher can use parent volunteers in addition to classroom volunteering. It helps if you clearly describe to parents what needs to be done and the time it will take. Offer parents choices about how they can serve their child's classroom.

Recruiting Volunteers

Make a list of all the possible places you might go to recruit volunteers for these tasks. You might include:

parents	senior citizens
peers	retired teachers
children in older classes	volunteer agencies
students from a nearby college or university	

The method of recruiting for each group will differ. Will you make a phone call, send a letter home, or attend a meeting of the group to explain your needs? Here is a sample letter:

Dear Senior Citizen,

Our kindergarten class needs volunteer help. We have a large, comfortable rocking chair and need volunteers at any time of the day to come in and read to individual children. Many of our children are not read to at home, so they really need someone to read just to them.

We could also use volunteers to write for the children who cannot write. You would have to be able to print what each child says about his or her pictures.

If you can volunteer, please complete this form.

Name: _____

Address: _____

Phone: _____

I volunteer to _____ read to a child.
              _____ write for a child.

Available: (circle times you are free)

Monday	morning	afternoon
Tuesday	morning	afternoon
Wednesday	morning	afternoon
Thursday	morning	afternoon
Friday	morning	afternoon

Do you need transportation?

_____ yes _____ no

It is better to start out small because each volunteer and aide will need orientation to understand the ground rules of your classroom, the expectations you have of the children and the adults, and the organization of your program. You might decide to have an orientation meeting for all of your volunteers and aides or to talk with each one individually. In some cases (like lap reading) you'll want to be sure there is a personality match between child and adult.

A volunteer should be asked to come in a bit early to get instructions, either verbal or written, and to take five minutes at the end to either tell you or write up what happened so that you can carefully monitor the work of the volunteer and express appreciation for the work done.

Training Aides and Volunteers

Aides and volunteers will need training. Even those who are former classroom teachers can use refresher points. How you train will depend upon the tasks you have the individuals do. You might hold a group meeting, give the volunteers a handout to read, or assign them some reading in a published work relating to the task at hand.

Some volunteers may never have worked with children or large groups of children the same age in the same room. Some need some preparation for the experiences they are about to encounter. An excellent idea, if the school facilities allow for it, is to videotape the class for a period. Then share the principles or theory about child development appropriate to the videotaped scenes in a training session. This introduces volunteers to the actual children with whom they will be working and provides background for all work with children.

Another example is that all volunteers interested in lap reading could read aloud to each other in pairs. The session could be taped and critiqued by the volunteers. If this proves too threatening, videotape yourself reading a lap story and point out good lap reading techniques.

Adults who do not read well should be encouraged to share other aspects of the book experience with children. Ask them what they feel comfortable doing. They could be paired with a reader to work with a small group of children, discussing the pictures after the first reading of the story. The ideal is to find a workable match between the volunteer's skills and abilities and your classroom needs. In any case, you will want to observe your aides and volunteers carefully during their initial visits as they build rapport so that you can see problems well before they become major.

A most important step is to introduce the volunteer to the classroom. This step must be well handled for the volunteer to be a success. How can this be accomplished? First, the guest should be introduced to the children and the purpose of the visit explained. If young children know that this person is volunteering to be with them and how appreciative you are of the help, they will be on their very best behavior for the class assistant. Likewise, a college intern is a teacher, not a pal, and deserves children's respect and cooperation. Second, there should be some observation time in the classroom. The purpose of this period is to give the adult a feel for this particular classroom and group of children. Awareness of the interaction of the group with respect to individual children and with respect to adults is important in order to respond intelligently to the individual child's behavior. Third, there should be some interaction time during which the adult is not expected to lead children, but to follow them. This should include time with the child or children with whom you expect to have them working. This allows the children to develop a sense of responsibility for the relationship, rather than leaving it all on the shoulders of the untrained adult or another child.

All of these steps give you time to assess the potential success of a particular volunteer and specific children. In addition, you'll make a judgment about the types of service that may be most appropriately done by each volunteer. Both the volunteer and the children have a chance to assess the situation before a commitment is made.

It is appropriate that *both* sides have some choice about working together. Volunteers deserve to know that it is the child's choice to be involved with them in this activity. By proceeding in this fashion you have circumvented many of your potential discipline problems. They are less likely to arise and are more easily handled if there is an underlying relationship established on a constructive basis.

What about the child who poses real problems in your classroom? You may have a volunteer suited to meet that child's need, but if you have no really good match for that child, *face it!* You, not the volunteer, must work with that child.

Be certain the volunteer understands and agrees to a professional relationship where individual children are not discussed outside the classroom. Fear of gossip and problems in home–school relationships have led some school districts to prohibit parents from volunteering in their own children's classroom. The opportunity for parent and teacher to work together and for the parent to learn more about the child's class environment is removed.

Giving Feedback to Aides and Volunteers

It is critically important to keep the communication between you and the volunteer open at all times. Write little notes back and forth. Praise what is good, be appreciative of the help, but be certain negative behaviors are corrected right at the beginning. Take time to observe the volunteer and to give feedback.

You should set up an ongoing reporting system to keep yourself aware of the quality of the experiences that the children and volunteers are having. Forms can be used by the volunteers as they leave (see fig. 19). These should be checked by you daily. If the program is to be constructive, you must be sensitive to adjustments that these reports indicate are needed.

One of the pleasant aspects of using volunteers is the freedom you have to offer children and adults several different experiences during the year. If a need or desire for a change is indicated, it can be made immediately. One way to facilitate such a change is through the regular meeting for volunteers. This offers an opportunity for them to share ideas, problems, and solutions, and discuss cooperative ventures. This experience may be a time to group volunteers who may be working with the same children at different times. It establishes an opportunity for additional training as you become aware of the need.

Expect progress to result from your volunteer program, and you will find it enhances your school program and your school's image in the community. Let your volunteers know that you expect to use their talents and that their role will grow as together you establish how they may best serve particular children's needs for individual attention and adult models.

Some Examples

At this point let us share some successful projects that have greatly enhanced early childhood litera-

ture programs. The Saturday workday, with teacher providing a snack or parents bringing picnics, has yielded a loft for one teacher that provides a nice quiet reading place in an otherwise crowded classroom; bookshelves and a room divider for the reading corner of another classroom; several book-related games for another teacher; and a puppet theatre for another room. The possibilities are infinite.

Saturday bake sales, garage sales, and car washes have yielded funds to buy books and sup-

---

Volunteer Report Form

Child _____ Date _____

Activity (What did you do?):

Evaluation (How did it work?):

Comments:

Figure 19. Volunteer report form.

port programs like RIF. Check to see if your school system allows fund-raising first. If classrooms can't raise money, often a PTA group can.

Volunteers have given a chalk talk to one class, made books with another, played guitar and sung in another, and told stories. Guests combined with field trips add spice to your routine. One parent who worked and could not come into the classroom took instructions home for making a classroom interest center and spent seven hours constructing it.

Regular classroom volunteers are valuable also. Be sure to let your regular volunteers know you are counting on them and that you will need to know in advance if they are unable to attend. One parent felt such a keen sense of responsibility to do her job that on a day when she had to remain home, she got a substitute!

One kindergarten teacher has a different parent arrive at 10 a.m. each day to write down the children's stories for them. The youngsters sign up ahead of time to go into the hall and have their stories written for them. Children await with eager anticipation the visit of "Grandpa Paul," who comes once a week to a day-care center and sits in a rocking chair telling stories.

In another kindergarten, fifth graders come weekly to read with their kindergarten "pals." Each pair finds a quiet place—usually outside—to sit comfortably and read a book. The fifth graders have practiced reading the book ahead of time. Fifth graders who don't have partners put on puppet shows for the class.

Benefits

Using aides and volunteers is time-consuming and demands organization and a change of role on your part. But if you gain more one-to-one help for the children, more variety in exposure to literature, more flexibility in your use of resources, it will be well worthwhile for the children.

Adults gain both the satisfaction of the relationship and that of having served the community. In addition, they are often able to gain from each other through the associations established with their peers. Parents glean tremendous insights into their children's experiences at school and often get ideas for working with their children at home as well. Older children gain opportunities for leadership that our age segregated schools rarely encourage. Cross-age tutoring programs

have shown that not only do the young children improve their attitudes toward and skill in reading, but the older children benefit by improved reading skill and self-concept.

However, you will want to build in some recognition beyond the intrinsic values of the experience. A dinner, a class party with awards, or a skit provide a time to extend special acknowledgment to the volunteers. A phone call or thank you note will be appreciated.

A Parent Corner

Teachers should give much thought to making their classroom environment a warm and welcoming one for parents. If parents are to lap read, is there a rocking chair, sofa, or other comfortable place with good lighting in which to read? Parents will not stay long to observe in the classroom if they don't have a comfortable place to sit. In many British schools a visitor is immediately offered tea and a tour.

Some teachers provide a lending library for parents, including parent education books. A list of recommended titles is included at the end of this chapter. A bulletin board for announcements for parents will also attract parents inside the classroom.

Involving Parents

Research has shown that family life exerts a lasting influence on children and that parental example is extremely influential in school success (Coleman, 1966; and Bullock, 1975). For these reasons, parents are encouraged to do things with their children that will cultivate exposure to books and a variety of reading experiences. Pleasurable contacts with books and magazines in the home can help a child develop a lasting love and respect for reading.

Parents who read with their child, who have books around the house as well as magazines and newspapers, who point out print on signs, who write and receive letters, etc., are immersing the child in printed literature of one kind or another and are doing a great deal to make reading a natural experience for that child. In contrast, the parent who never reads, who allows the child to watch hours of television, who constantly leaves the child with a neighbor or a sitter, or who does not value literature by his or her actions, will very likely have transmitted those values to the child. No matter what you do as a teacher with this latter student, the child is not likely to become an avid reader unless the parents change at least their attitudes—if not their behaviors.

Fortunately, you are working with young children at an age when habits and behaviors are still flexible. Thus, you must involve the parents in helping the child grow and learn. In everything you plan as a teacher, think about ways in which parents could support, aid, or otherwise benefit and enhance your teaching and make the child's learning more meaningful. Parents are your greatest allies in the effort to make literature the core of your curriculum.

Helping Parents Share Literature at Home

Involving parents in a literature program at home is far more natural and easy to implement than in many other areas of the curriculum. Many parents already read aloud to their children and are relatively comfortable with books. Unfortunately, the basic skills movement has influenced parent education programs so that many do not build upon this natural parent involvement, but rather have parents work with their children on "tasks" that teach isolated basic skills or attempt to teach reading (Freshour, 1972; Duncan and Vonbehren, 1974; McWilliams and Cunningham, 1976; Cassidy and Vukelich, 1978; Esworthy, 1979).

Workshops

Several parent education programs have focused on literature. Baker et al. (1975) taught a children's literature class for parents during which they showed parents how to supplement the work of the school. The class acquainted parents with a variety of materials and many avenues of reading enjoyment.

A classroom teacher might offer evening or Saturday workshops for parents. Make-it-take-it sessions could provide parents with puppets and props based on children's books to share with their children. Parents could learn how to read aloud effectively with their young children. They could be introduced to newly published children's books and share ideas together on involving their children with literature.

Workshops that involve parents are usually more valuable than lectures. Inviting a known guest speaker sometimes attracts more parents. Having a parent committee organize the workshop, select the topic, and inform other parents increases attendance.

Book Fairs

Houseman (1973) writes about a book fair that involved not only parents, but also grandparents and children who read and illustrated books together during the week of the fair. Book fairs can also be good times for "performances" related to books—skits, puppet shows, children reading aloud—similar to a music or dance concert.

Library Programs

The Children's Book Council (1979) funded six grants for proposals that increased parent participation in their children's reading. One library program invited employees from the high-rise office building surrounding a downtown public library to come during the lunch hour with their sack lunches to hear specialists talk about children's books, reading readiness, books for reluctant readers, etc.

Another funded program distributed packets to new mothers in hospital maternity wards. These packets contained a list of books for very young children, a small collection of finger plays, directions for making simple puppets, and an invitation to enroll their babies in the library's Toddler Story Hours, among other things.

Parents need to be informed about programs offered by public libraries and bookmobiles. If teachers take small groups from their classes to the public library and make sure each child has a library card, the children will often initiate further visits with their parents.

Communicating with Parents

Workshops, book fairs, and special events teach parents a lot about sharing literature with their children. Big events such as these take time to organize and plan. Equally effective are less formal methods for communicating with parents. Notes home can give suggestions.

Dear Parents,

    This week I have read aloud several stories from ___Winnie-the-Pooh___ by ___A. A. Milne___. The children have enjoyed listening to the stories, even though there are no large pictures with them.

You might want to borrow ____Winnie____ from the library or buy a copy from our bookclub next week.

Or you might send a note to an individual parent:

Dear Mrs. Long,

Jimmy has been so interested in babies since his little sister arrived that I found this book for him. It is a bit too hard for him to read by himself, so you'll have to read it to him. I hope you both enjoy it.

Sincerely,

At the end of the school year teachers often send home a summer calendar of activities or a booklet containing ideas for parents to use during the summer. A letter such as the one in figure 20 might be sent home.

Periodic communication, such as through a classroom newsletter, is another avenue for parent communication. One early childhood teacher sits in the middle of her classroom at a typewriter each Friday afternoon and asks the children what they'd like to report in the newsletter. Children share poems they have written, individual accomplishments, and announcements. The teacher has a section relating classroom news, both past and future, a column asking for help (we need spools for our collages; we need a parent to help us make books at 10 a.m. on Thursdays), and an idea for parents to try at home with their children. Since the newspaper arrives home regularly, parents can anticipate its arrival and read it.

Home Visits

One of the most effective ways to learn about children is to visit their homes and talk with their parents at home. You can observe the number and kinds of reading and writing materials in the home. Children like to plan ahead to show the teacher "their room." Home visits before the start of the school year make a nice introduction to school for the young child.

Books into the Home

Many teachers of young children give their students gifts at the end of the year or for a holiday. Inexpensive paperback books make excellent gifts that improve the home environment. Bookclubs

---

Dear Parents,

It's a fact that children in general spend more time in front of the TV than they do in school. During the summer when children are away from classrooms, this percentage of watching is probably increased in most homes.

You can help your children enjoy books and spend a profitable summer by developing habits of reading and sharing literature in your home and neighborhood. The following are some suggestions for a Summer Literature Experience.

Organize a neighborhood "read-in" time. Arrange with two or three other neighbors for round-robin reading and storytelling sessions several mornings a week. Rotate the sessions at different homes.

Organize a neighborhood treasure hunt to find a book.

Become backyard scientists by reading informational books and environmental materials about the natural habitat in everyone's backyard.

Try out a new recipe from a child's cookbook.

Plan a "chapter-a-day" for the whole family. Plan this before bed, over dessert at dinner, under a tree in the early evening, or with cereal for breakfast.

Set aside "Q-R-T" (Quiet Reading Time) every day whether it's looking at picture books for the nonreader or magazines for grandparents. Everyone reads!

Visit the public library together. Investigate records, filmstrips, puppet shows, story hours, and other activities and materials your library provides.

Sincerely,

Figure 20. Sample letter to parents.

(such as Scholastic) sometimes offer special rates for gift books.

Children, even if they are too young to write their names on the card, should have the opportunity to borrow books from the classroom library and school media center. One first grade teacher asks each parent to read aloud with his or her child for ten minutes a night. She gives each child a bookmark and sends a book home every night with each child. The benefits of that nightly reading have been many. By the end of the year, the children are intimately familiar with a great many books and authors. They have acquired a habit that is likely to carry over to summers and holidays.

We devote an entire chapter (chapter four) to the important topic of reading aloud. Much of the information in that chapter might be shared with parents. Likewise the activities cited in chapter three might give parents several ideas for extending literature experiences.

Summary

Since it is in the home where lifelong attitudes and habits originate, it is vital that early childhood teachers work closely with parents to capitalize on the home influences upon young children in their classes. Especially appropriate in the literature program is parent involvement because most parents of young children are already marginally involved.

There are several critical messages for parents. One is not to stop reading aloud to their children once the children have learned to read for themselves. Continue reading aloud as a family activity for sharing literature. Another message is to be supportive, not critical, of the beginning reader (correct as seldom as possible). Parents need to know that how they read to children is important. Reading and sharing literature needs to be a relaxed, spontaneous event, not a chore-like assignment or obligation. And, the purpose of sharing literature at home is enjoyment, not instruction.

Suggested References for Parents

Arbuthnot, Mary Hill. *Children's Reading in the Home.* New York: Lothrop, Lee & Shepard Books, 1969.

Berg, Lelia. *Reading and Loving.* London: Routledge and Kegan Paul, 1976.

Brogan, Peggy, and Clay, Marie. *Reading Begins at Home.* Auckland, New Zealand (and Exeter, N.H): Heinemann Educational Books, Inc., 1979.

Chan, Julie, M. T. *Why Read Aloud to Children?* Newark, Del.: International Reading Association, micromonograph, 1974.

Duff, Annis. *Bequest of Wings: A Family's Pleasure with Books.* New York: Viking Press, 1944.

Lamme, Linda, et al. *Raising Readers: A Guide to Sharing Literature with Young Children.* New York: Walker & Co., 1980.

Lanes, S. *Down the Rabbit Hole: Adventures and Misadventures in the Realm of Children's Literature.* New York: Atheneum Publishers, 1976.

Larrick, Nancy. *A Parent's Guide to Children's Reading.* 4th ed. New York: Doubleday & Co., Inc., 1975.

Let's Read Together: Books for Family Enjoyment. 3rd ed. Committee of National Congress of Parents and Teachers and Children's Services Division, American Library Association, eds. Chicago, 1969.

MacCann, D. *The Child's First Books.* New York: H. W. Wilson, 1973.

Opening Doors to Preschool Children and Their Parents. Chicago: American Library Association, 1977.

Reading with Your Child through Age 5. Children's Book Committee of the Child Study Association/Child Study Project Head Start. New York, 1972.

Rogers, Norma. *How Can I Help My Child Get Ready to Read?* Newark, Del.: International Reading Association, micromonograph, 1972.

Rogers, Norma. *What Books and Records Should I Get for My Preschooler?* Newark, Del.: International Reading Association, micromonograph, 1972.

Selection Aids for Parents

Cianciolo, Patricia, ed. *Picture Books for Children.* Chicago, Ill.: American Library Association, 1973.

Simmons, Beatrice, ed. *Paperback Books for Children.* Chicago, Ill.: American Library Association, 1972.

Sorensen, Marilou, ed. *What Shall We Read?* Logan, Utah: Utah Council of Teachers of English, 1979.

Subject Guide to Children's Books in Print. Detroit, Mich.: R. R. Bowker, Annual Edition.

White, Mary Lou. *Adventuring with Books: A Booklist for Pre-K—Grade 6.* Urbana, Ill.: National Council of Teachers of English, 1981.

Bibliography

Baker, Irving; Durdeck, Fran; Rowell, Elizabeth H.; and Schmitt, Mimi. "Children's Literature at Home Base." *Reading Teacher* 28 (1975): 770-772.

Breiling, Annette. "Using Parents as Teaching Partners." *Reading Teacher* 30 (1976): 187-192.

Brock, Henry C., III. *Parent Volunteer Programs in Early*

Childhood Education: A Practical Guide. Hamdon, Conn.: The Shoe String Press, 1976.

Bullock, Allan. *A Language for Life.* London, England: Her Majesty's Stationery Office, Department of Education and Science, 1975 (The Bullock Report).

Carter, Barbara, and Dapper, Gloria. *Organizing School Volunteer Programs.* Englewood Cliffs, N.J.: Scholastic Book Services, 1974.

Cassidy, Jack, and Vukelich, Carol. "Survival Reading for Parents and Kids: A Parent Education Program." *Reading Teacher* 31 (1978): 638-641.

Children's Book Council. "Getting Parents Involved in Books for Children." *Reading Teacher* 32 (1979): 822-825.

Coleman, James S., et al. *Equality of Educational Opportunity.* Washington, D.C.: U.S. Government Printing Office, 1966.

Criscuolo, Nicholas P. "Activities That Help Involve Parents in Reading." *Reading Teacher* 32 (1979): 417-419.

Duncan, Linda J., and Vonbehren, Barbara. "Pepper—A Spicy New Program." *Reading Teacher* 28 (1974): 180-183.

Esworthy, Helen Feaga. "Parents Attend Reading Clinic, Too." *Reading Teacher* 32 (1979): 831-834.

Freshour, Frank W. "Beginning Reading: Parents Can Help." *Reading Teacher* 25 (1972): 513-516.

Gartner, Alan; Kohler, Mary; and Riessman, Frank. *Children Teach Children.* New York: Harper & Row, Publishers, Inc., 1971.

Granowsky, Alvin; Middleton, Frances R.; and Mumford, Janice Hall. "Parents as Partners in Education." *Reading Teacher* 32 (1979): 826-830.

Houseman, Ann Lord. "Tuned in to the Entire Family—A Book Festival." *Reading Teacher* 27 (1973): 246-248.

Mastors, Charlotte. *School Volunteers: Who Needs Them?* Bloomington, Ind.: Phi Delta Kappa Educational Foundation, 1975.

McWilliams, David R., and Cunningham, Patricia M. "Project PEP." *Reading Teacher* 29 (1976): 653-655.

Miller, Bette L., and Wilmshurst, Ann L. *Parents and Volunteers in the Classroom: A Handbook for Teachers.* Palo Alto, Calif.: R & E Research Associates, Inc., 1975.

8 PRINT AND NONPRINT RESOURCES FOR A LITERATURE PROGRAM

Mary Elizabeth Wildberger
Montgomery County Schools, Maryland

"Hit the lights!" commands the six-year-old media assistant, and overhead lights dim, while the smiling faces of Frog and Toad appear on the screen. The children all know the "bluegrass" theme that signals another *Frog and Toad* story from the pen of Arnold Lobel, which is translated to filmstrip/record format by an independent media production company.

Various print and nonprint media resources are described in this chapter and strategies are given for using them with young children. Some children are more visually oriented; others are auditorily oriented. Some consider books as valued treasures; others prefer a movie or filmstrip. Your potential for reaching each child as well as expanding the opportunities for all children are greatly enhanced by effective utilization of media resources.

Sources of Nonprint Media

Nonprint media have run the gamut from novelty gimmick-riddled newness to their present status as an integral part of the school curriculum. Originally produced by a few educational corporations in science, language arts, and mathematics, the nonprint media have expanded their coverage to include guidance, art, and literature. There are review sections in the American Library Association publication *Booklist,* and *School Library Journal* publishes a separate magazine, *Previews,* devoted to the review of nonprint items. Magazines like *AV Instruction, Media and Methods,* and *Super-8 Filmmaker* are available in most public and school libraries and media centers for comparative "shopping" for both hardware and software.

AV Instruction is the official publication of the Association for Educational Communications and Technology, and is directed toward the school practitioner. Articles are reader-contributed and relate to the use of technology in an educational setting.

Media and Methods is a commercial newsletter with articles and reviews by well-known personalities and writers as well as by readers. Emphasis is on the current media scene and reviews range from new tapes of old radio shows to video systems.

Super-8 Filmmaking deals specifically with a single technology and includes articles on how to produce films, comparisons of available equipment, and suggestions for creative uses of this film medium.

Criteria for Selection

Considering the variety and availability of nonprint resources, it is important to establish criteria for evaluating these materials. Questions that might guide your selection follow.

1. Questions about the potential value of the materials:
   a. Are the format, vocabulary, concepts, and rate and methods of development appropriate for the intended audience?
   b. Will the material stimulate and maintain the user's interest?
   c. Will the user be stimulated to further study or discussion?
   d. Is it useful with individuals as well as groups?

e. Will it develop concepts that are difficult to get across in other ways?

f. Will it affect attitudes, build appreciations, develop critical thinking, or entertain?

g. Does it achieve its stated purpose?

2. Questions about the technical quality of the materials:

a. Is the choice and handling of visuals, composition, color, focus, special effects, etc., satisfactory and effective?

b. Are the visuals well produced and effectively used?

c. Are translations and retellings faithful to the original?

d. Are titles, captions, and explanations readable, of suitable length, and in proper positions?

e. Is the sound acceptable, with good fidelity, realistic sound effects, and absence of conflicts between the background music or sound effects and the narration or dialog?

f. If the media contain singing, are songs within young children's voice ranges?

g. Is the production imaginative and creative?

h. Are accompanying guides or notes well written and helpful?

Not all of the criteria will apply to each medium. These criteria, however, formulated in large part by the American Library Association, are workable benchmarks for assessing programs you might wish to use in developing a literature curriculum for young children.

Care of Equipment

It is important to give young children very precise directions about the use and care of audiovisual equipment. The teacher and media specialist model proper use. They should demonstrate how the equipment is used and have children practice under supervision before they use the equipment independently. A diagram or illustration can be a good reminder of proper care of equipment. For example, children need practice placing the record player arm carefully on the record, using the "pause" button, and replacing the needle carefully.

Children love awards. Simple certificates can be prepared and given to the child who demonstrates mastery of operation of a piece of equipment. The child retains the certificate and shows it as proof of competence to other students and teachers. One school uses the each-one-teach-one approach to teaching equipment operation. A child who has mastered the operation of a piece of equipment teaches another child until that child has mastered the technique. In this way many students can become responsible media assistants.

Miller-Brody Productions, with Random House School Division, has produced a set of A-V Equipment Self-Instruction Packets (School Service Dept. BL, 400 Hahn Rd., Westminster, MD 21157; 11 packets, each containing 1-3 cassettes, equipment diagrams, operating instructions, and teachers' notes. 1978. $209.79. #78287). The cassettes include information on handling, using, and caring for a variety of common types of audiovisual equipment. This set is a serviceable resource for busy teachers.

Films

Sixteen-millimeter films, ranging from Shakespeare to Maurice Sendak, are available for purchase and rental. Most school districts and day-care center offices have a central film library where films may be ordered from a county catalog. The media specialist in the school is able to book films for special units of study. In the nursery school or primary grades most films are literature-related. One prestigious film company in Connecticut (Weston Woods) produces *only* literature-based films. Morton Schindel, the director of Weston Woods Studio, has written:

> . . . the book and the film become companions in the communication process. Once the film has opened up the book to a child, he will want to hold it in his hands (perhaps upside down) and dwell to his heart's delight on the pictures that have some special meaning to him. His feelings about the motion in the picture will be reinforced.

A school system in Maryland has produced a catalog of motion pictures related to outstanding children's books. Funded with the assistance of the state educational agency and a federal grant, the project was designed to "encourage and improve children's reading through the use of literature-related motion pictures."

One valuable resource that mainly lists films and filmstrips produced in the seventies is Jill

May's *Films and Filmstrips for Language Arts: An Annotated Bibliography* (NCTE, 1981). This recent release concentrates on products suitable for ages 5-12; entries were chosen for their activity-generating potential and technical quality. Title, author, and subject indexes, and a list of producers and distributors, with addresses, are provided at the back of the book. These references can save the classroom teacher hours of research and screening.

Biographical films offer some interesting viewing. It is exciting to see film of an author or illustrator come to life on the screen, interspersed with film clips based on books that person has done. The Signature Collection (Weston Woods) is an example of this type of enrichment. In a sound filmstrip, Gail E. Haley discusses her technique of using wood and linoleum blocks to create a story's mood through illustration. In another sound filmstrip, Gerald McDermott narrates a program in which he discusses the design decisions that create the impact of his highly stylized artwork in the Japanese folktale *The Stonecutter*.

The Miller Brody series of sound filmstrips on Newbery Award-winning authors is an exciting experience for the child reader. When Arnold Lobel (of *Frog and Toad* fame) appears on the screen in his gorilla suit, young viewers react with spontaneous delight.

Nonnarrated films such as *Changes, Changes* or *Strega Nonna* are particularly effective in bringing an extra dimension to the printed page. All children can participate in this kind of viewing experience. Story involvement can be extended through discussion about the sequence of events in the story, predicting outcomes of the story, oral or written activities based on the nonnarrated film, pantomime, role play, or creative body movements.

"Reading" pictures on the screen is a vigorous involvement process, with children and teachers reacting to the visual stimulus. *The Bear and the Fly* by Paula Winter is now available in filmstrip format, as is *Bubble, Bubble* by Mercer Mayer, *A Flying Saucer Full of Spaghetti* by Fernando Krahn, and *The Silver Pony* by Lynd Ward.

An instructional television series, *Book, Look and Listen*, produced by the Maryland State Department of Education and distributed through the Agency for Instructional Television, has recognized this initial need for the child to "read pictures." In the first telelesson, viewers were asked,

"What pictures can *you* read? What sounds can you read?" Suggestions for extended activities and resources for the telelesson included these:

1. Discuss *Blue Bug's Safety Book*. Use magazines from which pupils cut out signs and labels that they can read. Each pupil may make a book to read to a friend or to take home.

2. Read the book *Gobble, Growl, Grunt* and have pupils supply the sounds for the pictures.

3. View a filmstrip without words with a group of pupils. Tape-record the story they tell to use as they view the filmstrip again. Use the same procedure with individual pupils as they "read" the pictures from favorite books.

Companies that produce literature-oriented films include:

BFA Educational Media
2211 Michigan Avenue
Box 1795
Santa Monica, California 90406

Contemporary/McGraw-Hill Films
1221 Avenue of the Americas
New York, New York 10020

Educational Enrichment Materials
(a company of the NY Times)
Dept. AN4
357 Adams Street
Bedford Hills, New York 10507

Encyclopedia Britannica Educational Corporation
425 North Michigan Avenue
Chicago, Illinois 60611

Films, Incorporated
1144 Wilmette Avenue
Wilmette, Illinois 60097

Learning Corporation of America
1350 Avenue of the Americas
New York, New York 10019

Miller Brody Productions
342 Madison Avenue
New York, New York 10017

National Film Board of Canada
1251 Avenue of the Americas
New York, New York 10020

Paramount/Oxford Films
5451 Marathon Street
Hollywood, California 90028

Phoenix Films, Inc.
470 Park Avenue South
New York, New York 10016

Pied Piper Productions
Box 320
Verdugo City, California 91046

Walt Disney Educational Media Company
500 South Buena Vista Drive
Burbank, California 91521

Weston Woods
Weston, Connecticut 06883

By checking with the media specialist, public librarian, or central film library in a school district, a teacher can enhance many of the delightful picture books shared in the classroom or media center. Myriad inservice programs and how-to demonstrations could be requested by teachers. The following checklist can be a helpful guide in sharing films and other nonprint media with young children.

Preview or screen a film or filmstrip first.

Make sure the equipment is in working order (bulbs bright, sound volume normal, screen in place, etc.)

Introduce the film to the children. Point out that the content of the film is familiar to them in book form.

Show the book on which the film is based.

View the film or filmstrip with the children.

Extend the experience in a classroom activity.

Filmstrips

The ubiquitous filmstrip, sometimes known irreverently as "ping movies" by the jaded second grader (referring to the advance signal), is enjoying a revival, due in part to the current educational awareness of multilingual literature resources. Filmstrips can be utilized in a number of ways. They can be used in an individual setting with a DuKane or other automatic projector/sound system. Filmstrips can come alive for young children and provide an "away-from-it-all" break when the child needs some private time. For the youngest preschooler, many favorite picture books have been translated into a filmstrip medium.

Filmstrips can also be used on an individual basis for a learning center. In one school, older children transcribe the sound tracks of stories into easy-vocabulary language, and write comprehension questions at the end of the filmstrip; that way first graders can be evaluated for comprehension skills.

In a group setting, an entire class can share the adventures of Charlotte, the spider, in a colorful, fast-paced filmstrip, and then draw pictures of their own spiders on U-film (unprocessed 35-mm film) and show their own versions of the delightful pig and spider fantasy. *The Wizard of Oz* provides a lively forty-minute special treat, and the Disney stories are available in varying lengths from the shortest *Three Little Pigs* to the lengthy *Snow White.* If Disney materials are used, it is important to also use other versions for comparison, since Disney has long been criticized in professional literature for watering down children's literature. (For a recent discussion, see Jill P. May, "Walt Disney's Interpretation of Children's Literature," *Language Arts* 58 (1981): 463-472.)

Filmstrips are an excellent method to study comparative folktales. Most commercial production companies have a generous list of folktales from all cultures. A teacher and media specialist can build a unit around a typical folktale theme, such as the "chase" theme (*The Gingerbread Man, The Three Little Pigs,* etc.), using print and nonprint media.

Filmstrips have an advantage for teacher–student involvement in that filmstrips can be self-paced. The operator is in control of the medium, unlike a 16-mm film, which rolls inexorably through the projector.

Filmstrips actually come closer to conveying the illustrator's intentions than any medium—except the book itself. Their versatility provides a natural communication medium between picture, storyteller (teacher) and child.

The most appropriate equipment for projecting sound filmstrips for individual or small group viewing is the rear-screen projector since the room need not be darkened for the presentation. A resourceful teacher can make a small theater from a heavy cardboard box from the grocery store. Tape white paper to the bottom of the box, put it on its side and "shoot" the image toward the bottom.

A group of teachers, when asked to complete the sentence, "I use a filmstrip . . ." came up with some inventive and exciting answers. Here are a few of them:

... as an independent center for one reading group, while I am giving a directed reading lesson to another. A "center card" with questions about the filmstrip must be answered by the group. The questions are about the story—the sequence of events, etc., so I can evaluate the children's comprehension. And it's usually total recall!

... to share a singing picture book. We show *Chicken Soup with Rice* (Sendak) while playing the Carole King recording of the song from the album *Really Rosie.*

... when the picture book we want to share is too small for all of the children to enjoy the illustrations. *Benjamin and Tulip* (Wells) or *Morris' Disappearing Bag* (Wells) can become a large group delight without losing the intimacy of the book.

Records and Cassette Tapes

Many teachers use records and cassette tapes to accompany a book or poem. Hearing an author's rich language read by a professional actor or actress brings a dimension to the book that silent reading alone does not provide. Sometimes teachers are reluctant to share poetry because they feel that their voices cannot properly convey the beauty of words. With records, the entire group can enjoy Shel Silverstein or Carl Sandburg and the teacher can benefit from the modeling that these poets provide.

Book/record sets are durable, inexpensive, and offer a wide variety of titles. Scholastic Book Services (904 Sylvan Avenue, Englewood Cliffs, New Jersey 07632) offers a catalog of record/book companion sets for preschool through grade 3 for eighty well-known picture books. Having the child just follow along as the story is read is an instructional experience in itself. However, some teachers of older children design simple followup sheets so that their record-and-book center can be an integral part of their literature and reading program. (See fig. 21.)

The Elves and the Shoemaker

A Study Guide

Before You Begin:

1. Draw an elf. Compare your drawing with those of other children and the elves Brinton Turkle drew for the book.
2. Discuss: What are elves? Are they real?

Listen to the story and follow in the book; then answer these questions:

1. What time did the elves arrive?
2. Why was the shoemaker able to buy more leather?
3. Why did the shoemaker and his wife make clothes and shoes for the elves?
4. How did the elves feel at the end of the story?
5. How did the shoemaker and his wife feel?

Extension Activities:

1. Buy and sell shoes at the shoe store in the dramatic play area.
2. Visit a cobbler, shoemaker, or shoe repair shop. Find out what shoes are made of in addition to leather.
3. Act out the story for other children in your class.
4. Study children's shoes in your classroom.
   Who has the biggest shoes? the smallest?
   Make a graph that shows how many children are wearing sneakers, sandals, laced shoes, and boots.
5. Make a collection of elf stories or elf illustrations.
6. Retell the story into a tape recorder.

(Littledale, Freya. *The Elves and the Shoemaker.* Illus. Brinton Turkle. New York: Scholastic, 1975).

Figure 21. Study guide for "The Elves and the Shoemaker"

Spoken Arts provides classic folktales and fairy tales in record or cassette format. Read by professional actors, the best-loved stories become a listening "experience" to fascinate the child.

English as a second language has provided the stimulus for listening to cassette tapes, either alone in a storytelling session or with the printed book. Many bilingual media programs are helping Spanish-speaking children enjoy the humor and pleasure of *Ferdinand* as well as helping them build a vocabulary and comprehension skillbank. Listening centers can pop up like mushrooms all over a school—in instructional areas, in the media center, and even in the school cafeteria! "Table tapes" help bridge the time between finishing lunch and going outdoors to recess. One chapter of *Homer Price* gives the child a new awareness of comic book heroes, like the "Super-Dooper" or skunk derring-do.

The most important value of book/record or book/cassette sets, however, is for the prereader to follow along and learn how to turn pages and follow print from left to right. Book/record listening is the closest thing a teacher can provide to lap reading, where a host of book awareness skills are learned.

Similarly, book/record combinations help the beginning reader learn visual and auditory word boundaries, a sight vocabulary, and voice fluctuations necessary for meaningful reading. The beginning reader can repeatedly listen to a story, memorize the story line, and then learn to match words to a story that he or she has already read and understood. As one beginning reader sighed in frustration while waiting for a teacher to read with her, "Oh, well, I guess I'll get Bill Martin to read to me." She was referring to the *Bill Martin Instant Readers*, published by Holt, Rinehart and Winston.

Videotape and Television

An assessment of the use of nonprint media in the literature program must include a brief discussion of television as a reading stimulus. Under ideal circumstances, when instructional television is used in the classroom, it is possible to evaluate its effectiveness in the cognitive area—learning letter formations, sounds of the long and short vowels, sequencing, and other measurable skills. *Sesame Street*, a Children's Television Workshop produc-

tion, has been funded to conduct this type of research. Papers appear regularly in the *Journal of Communication* evaluating its effectiveness in terms of measurable objectives.

Very little has been done to study the effect of instructional television in influencing students in the affective areas of reading self-selection skills. Measuring appreciation and enjoyment is much more difficult than measuring isolated skills, but in the long run it is far more important, especially if our goals for teaching are to develop readers, not just children who know how to read.

Perhaps Ezra Jack Keats has said it best with his analogy. In a recent talk at the Smithsonian Institution, the Caldecott Medal winner *(Snowy Day)* recalled his association as consultant to the production of *Sesame Street*. Mr. Keats remarked that the producers of the show had originally included selections from children's books as part of the program. However, *Sesame Street* researchers found that viewers' "attendant behavior"—that is, the fixed-eye-on-the-screen was not total during the literature segments, so the book selections were dropped from the program format. Mr. Keats felt that wandering eyes might be a "savoring" or "fantasizing" reaction to a lovely story rather than a lack of attention, but numbers and statistics prevailed. Mr. Keats concluded that an emphasis on teaching reading skills without providing the "reward" of a picture book or other selections from children's literature to read when the skill was learned was like taking the child to the edge of a cliff and dropping him over the edge!

A report by Joan Feeley, written as a presentation to the National Council of Teachers of English, was designed both to identify and describe the content interest pattern and media preferences of young school children. Feeley found that children "go to television to satisfy fantasy and entertainment needs and to print to satisfy informational needs." (Feeley, 1972).

Practical applications of television can be made at all levels when reading motivation is addressed. Influencing the reluctant reader, stimulating the timid learner, challenging the proficient reader, and extending the range of the print-oriented pupil are all practical uses of television for affective reasons.

Some schools now have production capacity as well as television monitors to receive commercial and public television. Combining the two can be an experience that children will cherish for years. One first grade class was experimenting with hatching chickens, during which the children shared "chicken" stories like *The Little Red Hen, Little Chick's Story,* and *Henny Penny* in dramatic role play or by sharing the pictures on camera. A videotape of this class period enriched the entire scientific process. When the baby chicks emerged from the eggs on videotape, the little producers nearly burst with excitement!

Many programs, like *Stories without Words, Book, Look and Listen, Spinning Stories, Once Upon a Town, Readalong,* and others are available through instructional television. Schedules for programming are generally available through the school media center or daily newspaper. Accompanying teacher guides are an enriching addition to the television viewing. Replay of programs telecast outside of the instructional day is generally permitted for seven days. It is a good idea to check copyright law before doing off-air copying.

Single Concept Films (Super 8)

Film loops or cartridges are available in commercial format (as opposed to home movies). Most of these stress specific skills and are not long enough for entire literary offerings, but are used by teachers to awaken the "imaginative eye" of the young child. Shown without sound, the emergence of the monarch butterfly becomes an exciting opening to a creative story or poem or an accompaniment to a children's book on the same topic. Seasons of the year can be brought to life in poetry or song by showing a single concept loop of a snowfall or the opening of a flower. A commercially prepared science loop can be used in literature units to accompany books on the same topics.

Microfiche

Picture books, easy readers, and thirteen full-length books are now available in microfiche format on 5×7 index cards. The card is slipped on the glass "stage" of a microfiche reader, and the book appears on the screen, page by page. "It's like personal television!" exclaimed one first grader, "and I can make it be any book I like best, too!"

Microfiche is good reading exercise for beginning readers. The children get the story line from the pictures, and their eyes follow from left to right on the microfiche reader, as they would if they were looking at pages of a book. In addition to eye movement, there is hand movement from left to right as the child guides the 'fiche through the viewer.

Study Prints

Collections of large, poster board pictures depicting scenes from fairy tales, nursery rhymes, poems, and interpersonal relationships are available as "study prints." This somewhat archaic title for a media genre frequently kills its popularity, except as bulletin board fillers, but the innovative teacher can find creative uses for these lovely pictures. A study print can be background for a finger puppet production; a series of nursery rhyme prints can provide a choral reading (speaking) experience for a shy group of youngsters; a group of fairy tale pictures can be placed in the center of the reading circle and individual children can select a picture and tell the story. It is helpful to rethink the uses of the abundance of media available.

Posters are frequently used as motivation for reading. The Children's Book Council (67 Irving Place, New York, New York 10003) offers a free catalog listing available free or low-cost materials. Caldecott-winning illustrators have designed bookmarks and posters, and other well-known illustrators of children's books have contributed their skills to the preparation of book promotional materials.

Many publishers offer posters and bookmarks that promote children's books and are usually willing to provide these materials in quantity if they are requested on school stationery.

One nursery school's walls were colorfully decorated with familiar characters from children's literature that were blown up to lifesize on an opaque projector and painted on poster board. Study prints, posters, and pictures can have both decorative and educational uses.

Student Productions

The student production can be an integral part of the media program. Children are encouraged to put their artistic and dramatic talents to work in role playing, while other children film the action, either with a Super-8 camera or the video camera. An instamatic camera or a Polaroid can be focused on objects of interest to children and the resulting photographs used as illustrations for child-authored books. Story extension can be encouraged by drawing pictures to illustrate a story such as *Harry, the Dirty Dog.* These can be produced as slides using a simple copystand (explained below), and then shown as a fullscreen production with accompanying tape. Creative stories based on a literature unit can be brought to the screen as television or movie programs. Hand drawn films and transparencies can be used over and over as part of a kit on folktales.

Child-authored books are a valuable addition to the print resources of a school media center or classroom library. These can be of two kinds: the dictated story (composed by the child, but written down by an older person) or the totally child-drawn and written story. The latter kind of literature is a very creative experience. The child author can tape-record the story and store the tape with the book in the library/media center. One school system sponsors an annual Write-a-Book Contest for children in the public schools. Entries are judged by children's book authors.

Illustrations for a child-authored book can be hand drawn, cut from magazines, or reproduced as photographs using a copystand. A copystand is a convenient piece of equipment for copying pictures. A camera is mounted on a rod, with lens facing down toward a wooden base. Lights are mounted on each side of the rod and directed toward the base of the stand. Artwork, magazine illustrations, realia, books, or other stationary materials are placed on the wooden base and photographed. A copystand can double as an animation stand for Super-8 film production. It is a no-fail device for the younger photographers and filmmakers.

Student productions added to the media center collection can be circulated throughout the school for curriculum use or can be shared with other schools or media centers. Many student film festivals are now held in school districts and states with categories open to kindergarten through third grade producers as well as to older children. Generally under the sponsorship of the professional media associations in the school district, the student showcase gives each child an opportunity to critique films produced by other children and compare different methods and techniques of film production. Museums, art galleries, and the American Film Institute are encouraging student filmmaking through courses in photography, Super-8 filmmaking, the preparation of slides, and the use of the visual marker and copystand.

Magazines for Your Classroom

Few early childhood teachers avail themselves of the multiple uses to which good children's magazines can be put in an early childhood classroom. You'll be surprised at how eagerly children anticipate the arrival of *Cricket* or *World* in the mail. Not only do you receive a continuing source of literature through such subscriptions, but also students learn how to use a periodical.

The stories and poems in magazines provide an additional source of literature to be read aloud—to groups and to individuals. The puzzles (which can be laminated with contact paper so that many children can try them) invite active participation. Magazines expose children to different genres of literature (short stories, fiction, true stories, poetry) and different styles of illustration.

Old magazines provide reusable resources. Try making a puzzle book, a recipe book, a poetry anthology, a collection of short stories, a joke book, or a song book from the better selections in old magazines. Color photographs can be used as wall decorations or to stimulate writing or storytelling.

Children can write (or have adults write for them) to authors, illustrators, or editors, thus integrating writing into the literature curriculum. Most children's magazines publish at least some child-authored and child-illustrated work. What better incentive for young children to learn to write and draw and to refine their efforts?

The quality of magazines for young children varies. So does the function of the magazine. Look for quality in the illustrations, in the content, and in the physical appearance of the periodical. A magazine that falls apart easily is not suitable for an early childhood classroom. We would recommend the following magazines.

Cricket Magazine is published monthly by the Open Court Publishing Company, 1058 Eighth Street, LaSalle, Illinois 61301. Features include short stories by well-known children's writers, nonfiction articles, poetry, puzzles, games, and reader contributions. Artwork is by prominent illustrators of children's books. Children's work is solicited.

World is published by the National Geographic Society, 17th and M Streets N.W., Washington, D.C. 20036. Features include outstanding color photographs to accompany well-written articles of a factual nature about our natural world.

Ranger Rick is published by the National Wildlife Federation, 8925 Leesburg Pike, Vienna, Virginia 22180. The magazine has a science and wildlife focus. Fiction as well as nonfiction is included. Regular features include photographic essays, craft ideas, and a monthly article on ecology.

Highlights for Children is published by Highlights for Children, 2300 West Fifth Avenue, P.O. Box 269, Columbus, Ohio 43216. It is an all-purpose magazine, including puzzles, stories, games, jokes, riddles, etc. Values are stressed in some articles.

Other magazines you might want to consider for your early childhood classroom include:

Children's Digest
Parents' Magazine Enterprises
Bergenfield, N.J. 07621

Children's Playmate
1100 Waterway Blvd.
Indianapolis, Ind. 46206

Stone Soup
P.O. Box 83
Santa Cruz, Calif. 95063

Ebony, Jr!
320 S. Michigan Ave.
Chicago, Ill. 60605

Humpty Dumpty
Parents' Magazine Enterprises
Bergenfield, N.J. 07621

WOW
Box 2007
Englewood, N.J. 07631

Bookclubs

Several companies now specialize in selling inexpensive books to children. The teacher is given free books for the classroom collection for every five or ten books the children buy. Slips are sent home periodically on which parents can check the books they would like to purchase for their children. The teacher collects the money and sends the order. The books usually arrive in a week or two.

Bookclubs that offer discounts on books and often screen the quality of the books they sell are an excellent way to increase the number of books children have at home and to expand your classroom library. However, care must be given not to "push" the books upon children or pressure parents into buying. Sometimes children who do not or cannot purchase books feel unhappy when the books arrive and there are none for them. An excellent way to deal with providing books for low-income children is to write for a RIF (Reading Is Fundamental) grant.

RIF was begun in the 1960s when Mrs. Robert McNamara discovered that when she gave a book to a child she was tutoring, his motivation to read increased dramatically. Now the federal government will subsidize free book distributions to every child over three in a classroom if the local group (PTA, etc.) will pay ten percent of the cost of the inexpensive paperbacks. The children must have free selection of the books and the teacher must have a program for reading motivation in order to obtain a grant. The address for RIF is c/o the Smithsonian Institution, L'Enfant 2500, Washington, D.C. 20560.

The pride of book ownership can go a long way to enhance a child's appreciation of literature and interest in reading. Book companies that operate through schools include:

Scholastic Book Services
904 Sylvan Avenue
Englewood Cliffs, N.J. 07632

My Weekly Reader Book Club
Xerox Education Publications
1250 Fairwood Avenue
P.O. Box 2639
Columbus, Ohio 43216

Nonprint Resources: A List of Professional Review Publications

Instructional Innovator (formerly *Audiovisual Instruction*)
1126 16th Street, N.W.
Washington, D.C. 20036

Horn Book ("Audiovisual Review")
Park Square Building
31 St. James Avenue
Boston, Mass. 02116

Instructor ("Reviews")
757 Third Avenue
New York, N.Y. 10017

Language Arts ("Staying on Top, Instructional
   Materials")
National Council of Teachers of English
1111 Kenyon Road
Urbana, Ill. 61801

Media and Methods ("Recommended")
North American Building
401 N. Broad Street
Philadelphia, Penn. 19108

Previews: Audiovisual Software Reviews
1180 Avenue of the Americas
New York, N.Y. 10036

Teacher ("Keeping Up")
Macmillan Professional Magazines
Greenwich, Conn. 06830

Today's Education ("Audiovisual Materials")
National Education Association
1201 16th Street, N.W.
Washington, D.C. 20036

Booklist
American Library Association
50 East Huron Street
Chicago, Ill. 60611

Bibliography

Feeley, Joan T. "Children's Content Interest—A Factor Analytic Study." Paper presented at the Annual Convention of the National Council of Teachers of English, Minneapolis, Minnesota, November 23-25, 1972.

Greene, Ellin, and Schoenfeld, Madalynne, eds. *A Multimedia Approach to Children's Literature: A Selective List of Films, Filmstrips, and Recordings Based on Children's Books.* Chicago: American Library Association, 1977. 2d ed.

May, Jill P. *Films and Filmstrips for Language Arts: An Annotated Bibliography.* Urbana, Ill.: National Council of Teachers of English, 1981.

9 SUMMARY

Linda Leonard Lamme
University of Florida

In this book we have tried to share with early childhood teachers many methods and materials for making literature the core of their early childhood curriculum. Some teachers may not be ready to dismiss packaged kits and basal series and design their own curricular units in the ways described here. The beauty of this approach, however, is that you can gradually adapt it to your existing classroom plans.

You might try using your basal programs three days a week and your literature program two days. Or you might reorganize your use of time each day so that literature can assume a more central role. Another approach might be to teach other content areas, such as science and social studies, from a literature base.

Some teachers take a topic (such as those discussed in chapter six) and then brainstorm all the ways literature could enrich that topic. Other teachers select a book and develop many curricular activities surrounding that book. *The Web,* published at the Ohio State University, gives many examples of "webbing" a curriculum around a specific book. The idea of webbing is to brainstorm as many ideas related to the book as possible. Then, the teacher selects from those ideas the best and most appropriate to use with the whole class, small groups within the class, and individual children. One must be careful not to overuse a book, making the resultant activities more important than the book itself. An example is given in figure 22 and the activity outlines that follow. It is contributed by Debi Frandsen, a student at the University of Utah. The book she has "webbed" is *Blueberries for Sal* by Robert McCloskey (New York: Viking, 1949, available in paperback).

Blueberries for Sal

I. Introduction
   A. Target Group: four to six year olds
   B. Objectives:
      1. To expose children to "good" literature.
      2. To present this literature through a variety of media so that children with a variety of modality preferences can enjoy it.
      3. To compile in this webbing various related ideas and activities, not all of which may be used at one time, in order that I may tailor the activities to the particular needs of the group I am teaching.
II. Literary Awareness
   A. Objectives
      1. Children will learn to go from basic recall to drawing conclusions from those facts.
      2. Children will be able to use imagination in creating new endings.
      3. The children may have the experience of recording their thoughts.
      4. The children will be introduced to the concept of plot and subject.
   B. Comprehension and Detail
      1. Why did little Sal's mother want blueberries?
      2. Where did they go?

Figure 22. Webbing for *Blueberries for Sal*.

3. How did little Sal get lost?

4. Who else was on Blueberry Hill?

C. Problem Solving

1. How are Little Bear and Little Sal alike? Different?

2. Why did Little Bear and his mother eat all their blueberries instead of taking them home with them?

3. What do bears do during the winter?

D. Critical Thinking

1. Read story up to the point where Little Sal starts looking for her mother. Have the children make up new endings.

2. Read the end of the story.

3. Which ending do you like best? Why?

4. Record new endings if desired. (See III, C.)

5. How many stories or plots are there in this book? How are they alike?

E. Interpretive Thinking

1. Objectives

a. The children will become accustomed to interpretive thinking.

b. The children will be made more aware of facial and body expressions.

c. The children will see the relation between movement and emotion.

d. The children will see that there are different reactions to emotions.

e. The children will use large and small motor skills.

2. Questions

a. How do you think Little Sal felt when she couldn't find her mother?

b. How did Little Bear's mother feel when she saw Sal?

c. How did Sal's mother feel when she saw that Sal wasn't behind her?

d. Can you make a surprised face? Scared face? Worried face?

e. How do you act when you're surprised?

(1) What does your body do?

(2) How do your arms react? Legs? Hands?

(3) What does your face look like?

(4) What does your mouth do? Eyes?

f. Have children go through magazines and find facial expressions and body expressions for surprised, scared, etc. Make individual pictures for each or a collage for each.

III. Language Arts

A. Objectives

1. To allow the child to use imagination and bring personal ideas into the discussion.

2. To involve the child personally.

3. To provide the child with a transition from pre-reading to reading.

4. To introduce the child to writing.

5. To teach the child to universalize the story from the book—it could happen to anyone.

6. To help children recognize the relationship between the spoken and written word.

B. New Endings

1. Read the story up to the point where Little Sal looks for her mother.

2. Have the children make up new endings and record them.

C. Experience Charts

1. Have the children make their own stories from experiences.

a. Have you ever been lost like Little Sal? What happened? How did you feel?

b. Have you ever gone for a walk in the woods or canyon?

2. As the children relate their stories, the teacher records them on a large piece of paper. This way, their initial introduction to reading is with materials written in their own words.

IV. Art Experiences

A. Objectives

1. The children have more than a two-dimensional art experience.

2. They become familiar with different media and textures.

3. The children can record what they saw and heard in a different media.

B. Collages

1. Make collage pictures of the story. Have the children pick out their favorite scene or character.

2. Have available a wide variety of materials. Suggested: buttons, twigs, leaves, rick rack, ribbon, fur scraps, fabric,

burlap, carpet scraps, sand, glitter, beads, etc.

C. Puppets
1. Make paper bag puppets. Materials needed: paper bags, construction paper, yarn, felt, fur, crayons.
2. Put on a puppet play. See Drama Experiences (V).
3. Objectives
   a. The children will be able to exercise their creativity.
   b. The children will learn how to manipulate the puppets.

D. Potato Printing
1. Have the children make potato prints with blueberry juice or blue paint.
2. Have the children cut the prints or choose the shapes desired.
3. Materials needed: juice or paint, paper, painting smocks, potatoes.
4. Start with blue, then add food colors—red, yellow, etc. What colors do you get?
5. Objectives
   a. The children use small motor skills.
   b. The children can see different shapes and designs.
   c. The children can see what colors mix.

V. Drama Experiences
A. Objectives
1. Through pantomime the child fulfills the need to pretend while at the same time developing a sense of "sensing."
2. The child becomes personally involved in the story.
3. The child, through creative dramatics, is able to better understand the characters and story without distracting and frustrating props.
4. The child learns sequencing.
5. The child learns critical thinking in critiquing the players' performances.

B. Pantomime
1. Let's go on a walk and pick blueberries like Little Sal. What kind of day is it? Smell the air. Is it hot or cold?
2. Let's go up a hill now. Do we have to walk differently? Are you getting out of breath? Do you see any berries? What do they grow on? What else can you see? What do you hear?

3. Let's pick some blueberries. What should we put them in? What would happen if we put them in our pockets? Has anyone tasted one yet? Taste it. Are they sweet or sour? How do they feel? Are they big or small?
4. Should we sit down and rest now? What are you sitting on? A rock, grass, pine needles, dirt? What does it feel like?

C. Creative Dramatics
1. Recall the story with the children.
2. Put it in sequence—what happens first, next, etc.
3. Go through the scenes.
4. Accept comments on how to improve it. Did Little Sal's mother act surprised?, etc.
5. Choose new players and reenact.

D. Puppet Plays
1. Put on a puppet play either following the story line or putting the characters in new situations.
2. Pick a situation and discuss how you think Little Sal will act.

VI. Sensory Experiences
A. Objectives
1. The child will have an opportunity to experience the book through different senses.
2. Through cooking the child will have the chance to manipulate utensils, use measurements, and eat.
3. The child will better understand how the body moves and will be able to move different ways.
4. The child will use comprehension and problem solving skills in comparing the sounds.

B. Taste
1. Taste blueberries. Are they sweet or sour?
2. Make blueberry muffins and taste test.

C. Movement
1. There are a lot of movement words in the story. Quote from story.
2. Can you hustle like Little Bear? How do you hustle?
3. How do you tramp?
4. Can you walk like Little Bear? Little Sal?
5. Is it easier on two legs or four?

D. Hearing Sounds
1. There are a lot of sounds in the story. Can anyone remember one?
   a. What about when Little Sal dropped blueberries in her pail—how did it sound? Try it. Would it sound different if she had a glass jar? A wicker basket? Experiment with the sounds. What if her pail was half full and then she dropped one in? Would it sound the same? Why or why not?
   b. Can you make the sound Little Bear made when he ate blueberries? Hustle, munch, and swallow.
   c. Can you remember who Little Sal found when she was looking for her mother? Can you make a crow sound?
2. Are sounds important in the story? When do they occur? (Help mothers find Little Sal and Little Bear.)

VII. Music Experiences
A. Objectives
1. The child puts the story in a totally different medium and learns to associate the two.
2. The children are introduced to rhythms and rhythm instruments.
3. The children will become more aware of the effects of music on conveying mood or creating a picture in their minds.
4. The children will demonstrate critical thinking in replaying the tape and revising it if necessary.
B. Music with Pantomime
1. Choose the music according to the moods of the story, characters, etc.
2. Tape the music together and play while the children pantomime. Does the music help explain the story?
C. Music as Accompaniment
1. Following the drama and movement experiences, the child should feel fairly comfortable with the movements and moods in the story. Now you can add the musical element.
   a. Discuss the tempo or speed of the story. Does it speed up or get more exciting when Sal gets lost? When she finds Little Bear's mother?

b. Discuss characters. What would Little Bear sound like when he's walking? Would it be fast or slow music? A high or low sound? Experiment—would Little Bear's mother sound louder or quieter? The same sound or different?
c. The children can pick out music or rhythms from recordings that fit the characters and moods. Then record them together. Read the story with the music as background.
d. The children can make individual sounds with rhythm instruments while you read the story. Tape and play back.
2. Discuss results. Does the music add to the story?

VIII. As a Supplement
1. Use this story as a supplement on a unit of colors.
2. Talk about the color blue.
   a. How does it make you feel?
   b. What does it make you think of?
   c. How would you move if you were blue?
3. Read the story and discuss.
4. Make a "blue" display along with other color displays.
5. Have the children bring special objects from home that are blue and let them make a display.

IX. Related Readings
A. Objectives
1. To lead the child into other books.
2. To help the child develop critical analysis—similarities in plot, etc.
3. To introduce the child to a specific author's works.
B. Suggested titles
1. *The Blueberry Pie Elf* by Jane Thayer.
2. *Are You My Mother?* by P. D. Eastman.
3. *Make Way for Ducklings* by Robert McCloskey.
4. *Time of Wonder* by Robert McCloskey.
5. *One Morning in Maine* by Robert McCloskey.
C. Possible Questions
1. Are there any similarities in these stories?
2. Can you tell anything about the author? Can you tell what part of the

country he lives in? Does he live in the city or country?

3. Show "The Art of Picturebooks" by Weston Woods (Robert McCloskey's interview).

X. References and Resources

A. Gilbert, Anne G. *Teaching the Three R's through Movement Experiences.* Minneapolis: Burgess Publishing Co., 1977.

B. Ross, Laura. *Hand Puppets: How to Make and Use Them.* New York: Lothrop, Lee & Shepard Books, 1969.

C. Strose, Susanne. *Potato Printing.* Little Craft Book Series New York: Sterling, 1968.

D. Huck, Charlotte S. *Children's Literature in the Elementary School.* New York: Holt, Rinehart and Winston, Inc., 1979.

E. Cullinan, Bernice E., and Carmichael, Carolyn W. *Literature and Young Children.* Urbana, Ill.: National Council of Teachers of English, 1977.

Assessing Your Literature Program

Whether you try the topical approach or the webbing approach with a single book, we hope that this book has given you many strategies for implementing an integrated approach to learning with literature at the core of the curriculum. It is important that as you move in the direction of integrated, meaningful teaching you assess your progress.

Several checklists have been presented earlier in the book that can be helpful in assessing your classroom environment and your skills at reading aloud to a group. By tape-recording your interactions with children (or videotaping yourself, if possible) you can discover your own strengths as a teacher and the areas that need improvement. In general, your classroom should be a more inviting place for young children and the children should be more integrally involved in learning if you have adopted the suggestions in this book.

Assessing the progress of the children in your classroom is important also. If the attitudes of the young children in your classroom are becoming more positive toward literature, you should see more children electing to read books, look at filmstrips, and act out stories during "free play" time. Children should more frequently request to read and be read to. They should make more references to books and story characters in the course of their daily work. They should use the library/media center more, both in school and at home. And they should request to read and be read to more at home. In other words, as their attitudes toward reading and literature become more positive, their behaviors should change and those changes should be observable both at home and in school.

You may also find it helpful to interview informally the children in your classroom or to question their parents to determine the effects of your literature curriculum. Parents may not think to tell you that their daughter mentioned, when she saw a boat being towed down the highway, "That's just like the boat Sal and Jane rode in to Buck's Harbor!" (from *One Morning in Maine*, by Robert McCloskey). But in the long run it is these references to literature in the context of daily activities that attest to the fact that children are becoming literate citizens.